Galloping Through History

Amazing True Horse Stories

Elizabeth MacLeod

annick press
toronto + new york + vancouver

We acknowledge the support of the Canada Council for the Arts, the Ontario Arts Council, and the Government of Canada through the Canada Book Fund (CBF) for our publishing activities.

**ONTARIO ARTS COUNCIL
CONSEIL DES ARTS DE L'ONTARIO**
an Ontario government agency
un organisme du gouvernement de l'Ontario

Cataloging in Publication

MacLeod, Elizabeth, author
     Galloping through history : amazing true horse stories / Elizabeth MacLeod.

Includes bibliographical references and index.
Issued in print and electronic formats.
ISBN 978-1-55451-700-8 (bound).–ISBN 978-1-55451-699-5 (pbk.).–
ISBN 978-1-55451-702-2 (pdf).–ISBN 978-1-55451-701-5 (html)

     1. Horses–Juvenile literature. 2. Animals and civilization–Juvenile literature.
3. Animals and history–Juvenile literature. I. Title.

SF302.M323 2015   j636.1   C2014-905002-X   C2014-905003-8

Distributed in Canada by:
Firefly Books Ltd.
50 Staples Avenue, Unit 1
Richmond Hill, ON L4B 0A7

Published in the U.S.A. by Annick Press (U.S.) Ltd.
Distributed in the U.S.A. by:
Firefly Books (U.S.) Inc.
P.O. Box 1338
Ellicott Station
Buffalo, NY 14205

Printed in China

Visit us at: www.annickpress.com
Also available in e-book format.
Please visit www.annickpress.com/ebooks.html for more details.
Or scan

Contents

v   Straight from the Horse's Mouth

1   BUCEPHALUS: The Most Famous Warhorse of the Ancient World

13 MUSTANGS: North America's Wild Horses

26 PATRIOTIC HORSE: Star, Unsung Hero of the Revolutionary War

39 THE PONY EXPRESS: Cross-Country Mail Movers

51 PIT PONIES: Fueling Industry from Deep Underground

61 SEABISCUIT: A Winner Against All Odds

72 Time Line
74 Horsing Around: Horsey Places to Visit
75 Main Sources
77 Further Reading
79 Photo Credits
79 Index
82 Acknowledgments

To Isabel, Lemuel, Augusta, and Cyrus—
for being animal lovers and distinguished
members of the family book club
—Michael and Michelle

Straight from the Horse's Mouth

They gallop and whinny their way into our hearts, and capture our imagination—but they have also changed history. Horses have done more to transform civilization than any other animal. Horses are the only four-legged animal that has changed the way humans live, travel, fight, work, and play. These strong, beautiful creatures have helped humans build and destroy countries and empires, and revolutionize the world.

There are more than 60 million horses in the world today. They take people where vehicles can't go, often for search-and-rescue missions, and they inspire us in ceremonies and parades. Of course people still enjoy riding them, as they first did more than 5,000 years ago. But in the past, horses did more than just move people. They carried armies to mighty conquests, pulled carts and wagons to move goods for sale, transported explorers across new lands, entertained millions, delivered regular mail as well as life-and-death messages, and much more.

Horses were there when some of the most important events in history took place:

- Meet Bucephalus, who carried the mighty leader Alexander the Great into battle and became the most famous horse of the ancient world.
- Read about the surprising origins of wild mustangs and their effect on the lifestyle of North America's Native people.
- Take a wild, stormy ride on Star, one of the horses that helped win the American Revolution.
- Join a Pony Express rider as his swift horse gallops along dangerous trails to deliver mail across the United States.
- Find out how pit ponies, deep in the earth's coal mines, helped provide the power to drive the Industrial Revolution.
- Discover the incredible story of the unlikely racehorse Seabiscuit and how he inspired a world in despair during the Great Depression.

The spirit, strength, grace, and beauty of horses have inspired conquerors, inventors, and artists. Riding a horse can give people a sense of freedom. Did you know that horses are one of the few animals that people do ride?

When we say that information comes "straight from the horse's mouth," we mean it's from the most reliable source possible. The saying comes from horse racing and means you can trust a tip about a race's winner because it comes from the best authority—the horse itself! You can also trust this fact: from tiny miniatures to huge draft breeds, horses have been vital to the development of nations around the world.

In the future, horses may not be used as much for work, but they will always be an important part of our lives and adventures.

Bucephalus

The Most Famous Warhorse of the Ancient World

Why is this incredible horse so wild, wondered Alexander as he watched the black stallion career around the field, throwing rider after rider. The boy was determined to ride Bucephalus, even though so many experienced horsemen had already failed to tame him. Just 12 years old, Alexander could be as stubborn and tenacious as any untrained horse.

But the stallion kept rearing up, shying at every rider. What was the secret to the horse's behavior? Alexander observed Bucephalus carefully. Unlike all the trained groomsmen there, the boy realized something was frightening the horse. What could it be?

If only Alexander could solve the mystery, this incredible beast would be his. Alexander's father had promised, and King Philip never went back on his word. The boy imagined riding the handsome animal into battle, at the head of a huge army.

Could Alexander detect something that none of the adults had been able to observe, and win the trust of this amazing horse?

THE UNRIDEABLE HORSE

On that sunny day in 344 BCE, King Philip of Macedonia, in southeast Europe, was scrutinizing Bucephalus (pronounced *Byoo-SEF-uh-less*) and all his would-be riders intently. So were many others. A lot of the men there knew that a famous soothsayer had once foretold to Philip, "He shall be king over the whole world and shall subject all to his power, whosoever shall leap upon the horse Bucephalus." Would the prophecy be fulfilled this day?

A horse breeder offered to sell Bucephalus to Philip for the high price of 16 talents—one talent was worth about 27 kilograms (60 pounds) of gold or silver. That meant the seller wanted more than 1 million dollars in today's money. Although the stallion stood out in the herd, that was an unusually high amount, nearly three times what other excellent horses might sell for.

But Bucephalus had been left alone with no one riding him for a long time and he had become unmanageable. Many of Philip's attendants had tried to mount the stallion, but he spun, kicked, and threw off the riders, no matter how experienced they were.

Philip became angry as, one after another, his men were made fools of by the horse. He had even tried to ride Bucephalus himself and failed. It was as if the horse were mocking him. Bucephalus was a handsome beast, but Philip decided that a horse that couldn't be ridden was worthless, no matter what the soothsayer had said.

Alexander was standing with his father, taking in all the action. An idea began to form in the boy's head, and just as the king was about to have Bucephalus led away, Alexander spoke up.

A Rough Ride

An ancient cavalryman had to be very athletic to get up on his horse's back. Saddles had no stirrups, or rings to hold a rider's feet. So a rider either needed another soldier to boost him up, a stone or stump of wood for a mounting block, or a spear to use as a pole vault. Some riders even taught their horses to kneel down.

Around 700 BCE, while most of the world—including men—was wearing robes and skirts, the nomads who rode their horses across the Eurasian plains pulled on trousers. The pants made sitting astride a horse easier and more comfortable, and they became popular around the world for riding.

THE CHALLENGE

"It is too bad that horse has been ruined," said Alexander to his father. "Those men do not know how to treat him."

"Whatever do you mean?" Philip asked, incredulous. "Do you criticize those who are older than you, as if you know more?"

"I could manage that horse better than they can," challenged Alexander stubbornly. He had noticed that Bucephalus didn't seem angry—he actually seemed scared. Not only did the boy see a distressed horse that was unsure of his handlers and so trusted no one, but he also saw a proud, intelligent beast. Alexander wanted to tame Bucephalus, and he thought he knew how to do it.

Philip admired Alexander's confidence, but he disliked his boastful attitude and decided to teach him a lesson. "If you can mount and ride Bucephalus, then I shall buy him for you," the king promised. "And if you don't manage him better," he continued, "what shall be your penalty?"

"I will pay the whole price for Bucephalus."

Loud shouts of laughter echoed in Alexander's ears. There was no way the boy could succeed when much more experienced horsemen had failed.

But Philip looked at Alexander thoughtfully. "If you can ride Bucephalus," he told his son, "he shall be yours."

The boy nodded, then grinned. He had a plan.

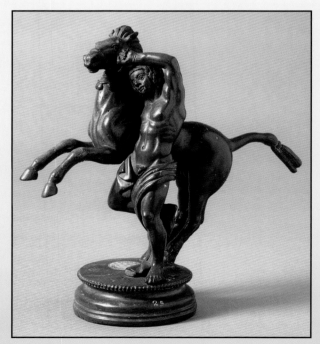

Alexander's strong relationship with Bucephalus has inspired sculptors, painters, and other artists.

FROM HORSE-BACK, IT WAS EASIER TO FIGHT WITH WEAPONS SUCH AS SWORDS AND LANCES, OR BOWS AND ARROWS.

KING OF THE WORLD

Alexander slowly approached Bucephalus. Gently but firmly, he tugged on the horse's bridle and turned him toward the sun.

What no one else had noticed was that, as mighty as the great horse was, he was afraid of his shadow. Every time Bucephalus caught a glimpse of the black shape that followed him everywhere, he reared up or tried to attack it. Alexander had observed that when Bucephalus was facing the sun he was much calmer. In that position, his shadow was behind him, where he couldn't see it.

Alexander whispered soothingly to Bucephalus and patted his strong neck. The great horse seemed to bend his head down to listen to the boy. After a few moments, Bucephalus quieted a little. The crowd gasped when Alexander swung himself up onto the broad back of "the unrideable horse."

The horse raced off across the grass. At first, Alexander couldn't control the great steed or make him slow down, but the boy stayed on. He didn't hit or whip Bucephalus as the other riders had. The horse galloped around and around the field. Eventually, when Bucephalus had tired himself out, Alexander reined him in and rode over to where his father was still standing. The crowd clapped and cheered, even the riders who'd been defeated by the wild horse.

It was then that Philip remembered the soothsayer's prediction about the greatness of the rider who could tame Bucephalus. "O my son," said Philip, proudly, "look thee out a kingdom equal to and worthy of thyself, for Macedonia is too little for thee."

The legend of Alexander the Great and his mighty horse Bucephalus had begun.

OX HEAD

Like so much about Bucephalus, how he was named is now lost in myth. His name means "ox head" in Greek, and some ancient sources say Bucephalus had a white mark on his forehead in the shape of an ox's head. Others say the mark or brand was on Bucephalus's haunch (upper back leg) and was shaped like an ox's horns.

This coin showing Bucephalus is likely about 2,300 years old.

There are also stories that Bucephalus had a large, heavy head shaped like that of an ox. As well, Bucephalus was obviously stubborn—or, as people used to say, ox-headed, and perhaps this is how he was named.

Although Bucephalus is usually described as a tall, black horse, experts today think that he likely had a reddish-brown coat with a black mane, tail, and legs; this coloring is known as bay (see page 35). Bucephalus also likely wasn't very tall, based on what historians now know about the horses that King Philip's army rode. These horses were known for their speed, strength, and endurance, and for having long lives— all characteristics important for warhorses.

When Bucephalus was tamed by Alexander, the horse was already about 12 years old. That's middle-aged for a horse, so the price his owner was demanding might have seemed especially high. But older horses have proven their ability to withstand hardships. They are less flighty than young horses, thanks to their tough experiences.

A STRONG BOND

When Alexander was just 20, his father was assassinated and the young man became king. The scheming rulers of surrounding countries and empires thought they could take advantage of Alexander's inexperience and expand their

ANCIENT GREEKS HAD MANY MYTHS ABOUT BUCEPHALUS. OTHER MYTHICAL GREEK HORSES INCLUDE THE TROJAN HORSE, PEGASUS, AND CENTAURS.

It was tough for early soldiers to stay on the wide, slippery, and sweaty back of a war-horse. Saddles weren't invented until around 750 BCE in Assyria (today's northern Iraq). And they weren't necessarily built for comfort. Some were covered in so much gold—to show how wealthy the rider was—that they were very difficult to sit on.

Saddles made controlling a horse much easier. But horses were still thought to be very wild and difficult to ride, so women weren't allowed near them, even far from the battlefield.

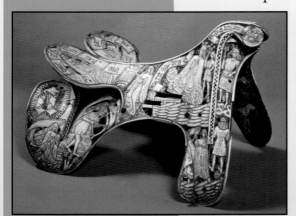

This saddle from about 600 years ago looks beautiful with its ivory decorations, but it would have been very uncomfortable to sit on.

kingdoms at his expense. So they waged battle on the borders of the new king's territory.

While Philip had often used diplomacy to settle disputes, Alexander preferred armed combat. He rode Bucephalus into war, the horse biting and kicking his foes on the battlefield. He would dodge and twist through the conflicts, one moment swerving away from an opponent's sword, the next dashing forward to attack. Alexander and Bucephalus had a special, close relationship and the horse seemed to anticipate his master's commands. Bucephalus appeared as fearless as Alexander, as well as calm in even the bloodiest battles.

Alexander took good care of his horse. Despite how tough Bucephalus and other warhorses of the day were, it was difficult for them to endure the extreme climate changes as they were marched from rugged mountains to burning deserts, carrying troops. Alexander always tried to give Bucephalus time to acclimatize before riding him into battle. Sharp rocks bruised and split Bucephalus's hooves, but sometimes Alexander couldn't let his cherished companion rest long enough to let his gashes heal before the battle trumpets sounded again.

THE LOYAL HORSE

Once, after Bucephalus was wounded in a conflict, Alexander decided to send the great horse away from the battlefield so he could be treated. But Bucephalus sensed the battle wasn't over and wouldn't allow Alexander to dismount. Perhaps he was jealous that the king was going to mount another horse. No matter how Alexander's men tried to calm Bucephalus, he would not allow the king to get down.

Bucephalus would let almost anyone ride him to exercise him when Alexander was away, or to bring him from the stable so the king could then ride him. But if Bucephalus was wearing Alexander's royal saddle and bridle and was equipped for battle, then the horse would allow no one to mount him except the powerful leader.

Later, Alexander repaid his horse's loyalty. When he was exploring new territory near the Caspian Sea (between today's Russia and Iran) with most of his army, he left the horses back in camp to rest. But raiders crept into the settlement and stole all of them, including Bucephalus.

Alexander was enraged when he discovered what had happened. He was certain that to the thieves, Bucephalus would look like any old horse. Alexander knew his brave mount could end up as an overworked beast of burden and the thought made him furious.

Yelling and cursing, Alexander vowed to destroy the entire country and kill all its people unless Bucephalus was returned to him. The thieves realized how much the king loved his horse and had no doubt he would carry out his threat. Bucephalus was quickly returned to his master. The thieves surrendered all of their cities to Alexander as well. Alexander was so relieved to have Bucephalus back that he treated the raiders kindly and—much to their astonishment—even paid them a reward for the safe return of his horse.

ALEXANDER THE GREAT

By the time Alexander was 25 years old, he and Bucephalus had conquered a vast kingdom. Bucephalus had shown himself to be not only fast but also tough, able to march great distances across rough terrain and still have the energy left to charge into battle.

ABOUT 2,000 YEARS AGO, CAVALRYMEN BEGAN TRAINING FOR BATTLE BY HUNTING OR PLAYING POLO.

Throughout 13 years of almost constant fighting, Alexander never lost a battle, even though he and his men were usually outnumbered. No wonder people were soon calling this successful leader "Alexander the Great." When he led a charge into battle mounted on Bucephalus, he inspired his soldiers—and frightened his enemies.

A LONG-LIVED HORSE

Alexander rode Bucephalus for almost 18 years. No one knows for sure how this valiant charger died. Some reports say Bucephalus died of old age when he was 30. Even today, that would be a good age for a pampered horse with an easier life than Bucephalus had.

Some experts believe the horse met a different end. Ancient reports tell how at the Battle of the River Hydaspes (in modern-day Pakistan) in 326 BCE, Bucephalus disobeyed Alexander for the first—and last—time. When combat began, the brave horse, with Alexander on his back, charged into the thick of the conflict, kicking and biting at any enemy horse who challenged him.

Suddenly, though, the famous horse turned and began running off the battlefield. Nothing Alexander could do would stop him and the furious commander could not get Bucephalus to return to battle. Finally, when the noble stallion was satisfied that Alexander was out of range of the enemy's weapons, Bucephalus stumbled and Alexander quickly dismounted.

It was only then that Alexander saw the terrible wound that Bucephalus had suffered in battle. Despite horrendous loss of blood, Bucephalus had been determined to last long enough to carry his beloved master to safety. It was only

Huns and Mongols on Horseback

Around 250 CE, fierce cavalrymen known as Huns galloped out of Central Asia to invade China. The Chinese kept them out with their Great Wall, so the Huns began attacking Europe. Thanks to their tough little horses, they conquered an empire stretching across much of today's Germany, Poland, and Russia. But when their leader, Attila the Hun, died in 453, the empire splintered.

In the early 1200s, Genghis Khan led Mongol soldiers on horseback out of Central Asia. With rapid cavalry charges these skilled riders conquered the largest land empire ever, across much of Europe and Asia.

Galloping Through History

Brave Knights and Strong Steeds

In many European languages—except English—the word for knight means "horse-man." That's because a knight's most important equipment was his horse. After all, a man in a heavy metal suit couldn't run very fast or very far.

Knights in armor first appeared on battlefields in the late 1200s in Europe, battling Genghis Khan's Mongol army. Their armor weighed almost as much as they did, so the fastest their horses could charge was about 24 kilometers (15 miles) per hour. That's about one-third as fast as a racehorse can run!

Horses wore padding or quilted fabric under their armor for protection and comfort.

when Bucephalus knew he had saved Alexander that the legendary stallion finally collapsed.

Alexander was heartbroken when his courageous companion died. The grieving leader insisted on holding a large, public funeral in honor of Bucephalus.

WARHORSES

Many historians say horses were the first "weapon of mass destruction," since they allowed armies to ride into built-up areas and wipe out entire cultures. For thousands of years, fighting was a horse's most important job, and in parts of Asia, Europe, and North Africa, it was a horse's only job. Oxen, mules, and water buffalo did the everyday work of plowing and hauling.

It was likely around 2500 BCE that soldiers on the plains of what is now southern Russia and west-central Asia

Alexander and his soldiers easily defeated Persia's King Darius and his army, despite Darius's warhorses and chariots.

first rode into battle in small two-wheeled chariots. Horses increased the speed of battle, allowing armies to carry out a swift raid and make a furious charge at an enemy's lines, or beat a hasty retreat. Sometimes, just the sight of a galloping warhorse was enough to panic a foot soldier.

Tribes who knew how to use horses in warfare had a great advantage over nations fighting on foot. By about 1000 BCE, every army was using horse-drawn chariots. While these vehicles made charges faster, they were unsteady and fragile. By 900 BCE, soldiers had learned to fight on horseback. They could outrun and outmaneuver enemies in chariots, and helped tribes like the Huns and Mongols from Asia conquer huge empires with high-speed attacks.

Meanwhile, in Europe, a different type of warfare was developing. In the late 1200s CE, knights began strapping on heavy metal armor. Then they were lifted up onto their strong horses, which were also wearing armor. The encounters between battling knights were one-on-one as the horses charged at each other and the knights tried to unseat or kill their opponents with lances and other weapons made for use from horseback.

Warfare changed again in the 1300s, when gunpowder began fueling muskets and cannons. Now foot soldiers had the advantage over charging cavalry, since they could aim their guns more accurately standing on solid ground than soldiers on charging horses could. Horses were used less and less in actual conflict, but were still important on the sidelines for transportation. World War I was the last major war that included horses in battle.

Marengo, Copenhagen, and Traveller

Many great military leaders have depended on brave horses. Napoleon Bonaparte, emperor of France in the early 1800s, set off to conquer Europe on his strong little horse, Marengo. In 1815, Napoleon was finally defeated by England's Duke of Wellington, who was riding Copenhagen, a horse known for his energy and obedience.

Robert E. Lee was the top Confederate general in the American Civil War (1861–65). He relied on the courage and endurance of his horse, Traveller.

ALEXANDER NAMED A CITY IN PAKISTAN BUCEPHALA AFTER HIS BELOVED HORSE.

BUCEPHALUS AND ALEXANDER, CONQUERORS

The king and his horse conquered countries from Greece in the west to Egypt in the south and as far east as Afghanistan, making the small kingdom of Macedonia the most powerful state in the world.

When Alexander died, his empire was the largest of its time: it stretched across three continents. For his part in this feat, Bucephalus became the most famous horse of the ancient world—some say he's the best-known horse ever.

Horses in World War I

Cavalry charges became outdated in World War I, but horses still pulled carts, delivered messages, carried soldiers scouting out enemy positions, and hauled cannons. The animals could traverse rough terrain better than cars or trucks.

Horses also boosted soldiers' morale. Some people estimate that a total of about 8 million horses from both sides served in World War I. Since then, tanks and machine guns have made horses obsolete in most battles, but they're still used in conflicts in some less-developed countries.

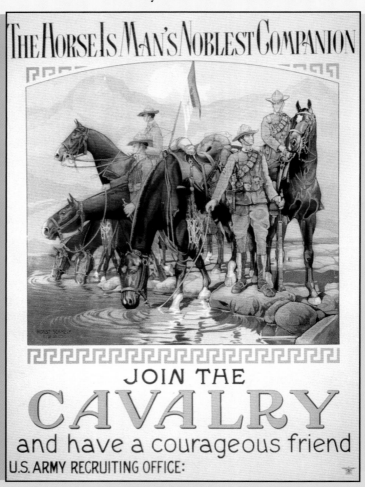

THE HORSE IS MAN'S NOBLEST COMPANION

JOIN THE CAVALRY and have a courageous friend

U.S. ARMY RECRUITING OFFICE:

Mustangs

North America's Wild Horses

The buffalo horses neighed as they galloped around the meadow. Chogan could have watched them for hours. He knew only the fastest, most agile mustangs became "buffalo horses"—the ones the braves rode to hunt buffalo. The mustangs seemed so proud as they tossed their heads and swished their tails.

Chogan's name meant "blackbird" in the Blackfoot culture, so it's no surprise that he dreamed of flying—but not with wings. Chogan yearned to fly across the plains on the back of one of his tribe's mustangs. His favorite horse was Koko (it means "night"), a jet-black mare with a small white patch gleaming on her face.

He was still a boy but Chogan imagined the day when he would ride one of these strong little mustangs. He had watched the Blackfoot braves preparing for the buffalo hunt and hoped the time would come soon when he would help catch the huge creatures that provided meat and leather for his tribe. Chogan wanted to ride a buffalo horse and prove himself a courageous Blackfoot.

THE CHIEF DECIDES

Chief Mingan (Gray Wolf) noticed that his tribe's supply of buffalo meat was low and his people needed new buffalo-skin robes for the coming winter. It was time to send his braves on a buffalo hunt.

Mingan called the men together to mount up. Then he spied Chogan watching the buffalo horses intently.

"Chogan," the chief called out. "You are ready to join the buffalo hunters. You will ride Rowtag."

Chogan couldn't believe his luck. He was going to ride with the buffalo hunters! The boy raced to saddle up before the chief could change his mind. Today, the braves would ride out to locate a herd of buffalo. If Chogan did well, perhaps he'd be able to join them for the real hunt tomorrow. Rowtag's name meant "fire"—the solid little mustang had a reddish-brown coat. Chogan clambered up on his back and joined the other hunters.

Koko was a strong, tough little mare. Like most mustangs, she could run like the wind.

It didn't take Chogan long to spot Koko in the crowd of horses and riders. Apisi (Coyote) was riding her, as he usually did. As the group trotted out of camp, Chogan edged closer. If he couldn't ride Koko, at least he could ride near her.

Apisi noticed the young man watching Koko.

"She's a good horse," said the older man, patting his mount.

"The best," agreed Chogan. Koko and Rowtag easily picked their way over the rough ground, thanks to their strong hooves and legs. Chogan

HEINRICH HARDER

kept a careful eye out for prairie-dog holes. He knew they could trip a horse and throw the rider.

As they rode along, Apisi told Chogan about buffalo and how to hunt them. But it was the stories about the mustangs that Chogan really wanted to hear.

THE WAYS OF THE MUSTANG

"Mustangs aren't like antelope or deer or other wild animals," Apisi said. "They're strong and spirited, but they can be trained. It's tough work, though. I remember the first time I lassoed a mustang and began training it. He bucked and kicked and sent me flying when I tried to ride him. I can still feel the sharp rocks I landed on.

"It didn't take me long," continued Apisi, "to learn why the smart braves train mustangs in ponds and creeks or on marshy ground—the landing's a lot softer!

"Once you train mustangs, they're loyal and obedient," he added. "They've got amazing

MUSTANGS

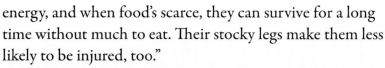

energy, and when food's scarce, they can survive for a long time without much to eat. Their stocky legs make them less likely to be injured, too."

"Are mustangs smart?" asked Chogan.

"Of course! One night I got separated from the rest of the braves. I was far from camp and the moon was hidden by the clouds. I had no idea where home was. Koko seemed to know where she was going. At one point, I tried to turn her to follow a different path, but she refused. Stopped right there and wouldn't budge.

"Just then, the clouds cleared for a moment and what I saw made my hair stand on end. We were right on the edge of a cliff! I was lucky Koko was too smart to obey me that time. Mustangs know when coyotes are hiding nearby, too, and—"

Suddenly, there was a signal from the leader, Machk (Bear), and the braves all became silent.

Sometimes Native scouts rode out at night to locate buffalo herds. The dark skies made it harder for the animals to see the scouts.

Galloping Through History

FINDING THE HERD

Apisi had already told Chogan that when the group came close to a watering hole or meadow where the huge animals might gather, they'd have to be careful to stay downwind so the buffalo wouldn't catch the scent of the humans or their mounts.

Machk tested the breeze and headed the hunters in a slightly different direction. Apisi now told Chogan how long-ago braves rode their mustangs bareback, with no bridle or saddle. To hold on, they clung to braids woven into their horses' manes. Later, the Blackfoot people learned to create bridles and saddles.

The hunters had just come around a small hill when Machk stopped them. There in the distance was a large herd of buffalo. There was plenty of grass, so they'd still be there tomorrow when the buffalo hunters returned. Silently, they turned their mustangs around and started on the trek back to camp to prepare for the hunt.

THE HUNT IS ON!

Early on the morning of the chase, the buffalo horses were decorated by the Blackfoot women with symbols of good luck. These would encourage the braves and ensure their success.

The chief began matching up the riders with the horses. About half the horses had been assigned when the chief finally turned to young Chogan.

"Chogan, you shall ride—" The chief paused and Chogan held his breath. *Please say Koko,* he thought.

"You shall ride Rowtag on this day as well."

Chogan's heart sank. "Yes, Chief Mingan," said Chogan woodenly. He knew he couldn't argue.

Sky Dogs

The Blackfoot tell the legend of the Sky Dogs to explain how the horse came to their ancestors.

Long ago, the Blackfoot saw three odd creatures coming from west of the mountains, from the sleeping room of Old Man, the Creator. The animals were as big as elk but delicate and beautiful. Two of the Sky Dogs each had a dying man sprawled across its back. The third pulled a *travois* containing a deathly ill woman.

The men soon died, but eventually the woman recovered and taught the Blackfoot how to train and care for the Sky Dogs.

IN THE WILD, MUSTANGS LIVE ABOUT 18 YEARS. DOMESTICATED MUSTANGS CAN LIVE UP TO 30 YEARS.

Return of the Horse

After horses became extinct in North America more than 7,500 years ago, they didn't return until 1493, when Christopher Columbus sailed from Spain to what he called the New World, bringing horses for a settlement in what is now the Dominican Republic.

Spanish explorer Hernán Cortés brought horses to Mexico in the early 1500s. And when Hernando de Soto, also from Spain, explored Florida and farther north, some of his horses escaped. Those horses, and runaways from early settlements, became a single group known as mustangs.

The Blackfoot were first introduced to mustangs in the early 1700s, likely by another tribe. The animals frightened and amazed them, but soon they admired the horses for their stamina and endurance.

But Apisi was watching Chogan and saw the boy's disappointment. He had impressed Apisi with his eagerness to learn and his lack of complaining during the long ride yesterday. Apisi knew which horse Chogan wanted to ride. But could he convince the chief to change his mind?

"One moment, Chief," said Apisi. "I brought down the greatest number of buffalo in our last hunt. I claim the right to choose my horse for this hunt. And I choose Rowtag. Let Chogan ride Koko."

Chogan's heart was pounding. Would the chief grant Apisi's demand?

The chief eyed the young man and the older brave.

"So be it," Mingan announced. "Apisi will ride Rowtag and Chogan shall have Koko. Now mount your horses!"

Chogan couldn't believe it. He would finally get to ride Koko! He raced to her side and jumped up into her saddle. "Let's go, Koko," he whooped happily.

The buffalo horses and their riders lined up, some men clutching bows and arrows, others carrying spears. At a signal from their leader they rode out of camp. When they were close to

where they'd seen the herd yesterday, they slowed and moved cautiously toward them. Suddenly, the leader gave a yell, and the horses and riders swooped down around the buffalo.

"Stay close to me," yelled Apisi to Chogan, "and do exactly what I tell you."

KOKO AND CHOGAN TO THE RESCUE

Chogan urged Koko forward. He watched as Apisi picked out his buffalo, then maneuvered Rowtag over to its right side—most hunters preferred to approach from this direction, Chogan had learned yesterday. Rowtag wheeled and spun, avoiding the other buffalo and keeping Apisi close to his target.

The little horse galloped in close to the huge, shaggy beast, near enough for Apisi to let fly an arrow. Apisi tucked the reins into the waist of his pants and, guiding Apisi only with his knees and feet, aimed his bow and arrow. His shot hit the buffalo just behind the head.

While hunting, Native braves relied on their mustangs to get them close to the huge buffalo.

HORSES' EYES ARE ON EITHER SIDE OF THEIR HEAD. THAT HELPS THEM SEE ALMOST ALL THE WAY AROUND THEIR ENTIRE BODY.

Immediately Rowtag veered away from the wounded buffalo in case it turned to attack. Meanwhile, Apisi shot another arrow. But the brave was focusing so hard on that buffalo, he didn't see another suddenly change direction and hurtle along menacingly—right at Rowtag!

"Look out," shouted Chogan. He dropped his reins and brought his bow to his shoulder. Koko didn't hesitate for a moment, but kept on steadily pounding across the plain so Chogan could get his shot away. Bull's-eye! The young man quickly fired off two more arrows to make sure the animal was down.

Apisi rode over to Chogan. "Good shot," said the older brave. "Now let's see if you and Koko can get another buffalo."

AROUND THE CAMPFIRE

The late-afternoon sun was low in the sky when the buffalo hunters and their horses finally returned to camp. The pack horses were heavily laden with meat and skins.

That night, after a celebration feast, the Blackfoot gathered around the campfire to hear Chief Mingan's stories

Galloping Through History

of long ago. Chogan glanced over at Koko grazing nearby. Buffalo horses were so valuable that at night they were kept very close to the tepees, where they would be protected from predators like coyotes and mountain lions—and other tribes that might try to steal them.

Mingan began. The buffalo hunt is an important event, he said. Success in the hunt meant the people would be healthy and strong. Failure meant starvation. Buffalo aren't very bright, admitted Mingan, but they're fast. Even worse, they are bad-tempered. And they're enormous, weighing up to 1,000 kilograms (2,200 pounds). So hunting buffalo has always been extremely dangerous.

In days gone by, braves camouflaged themselves in buffalo skins from previous hunts to mask their human scent, as well as to blend in with the hairy beasts. Crawling carefully, the braves crept closer and closer to the herd. There were times when they had to wait for hours under the heavy, hot skins for a chance to aim their arrows. The sweat poured off their faces and their muscles cramped. It took a long time, and often the men returned to the camp without a single buffalo.

There was another more common but much more dangerous way to hunt buffalo, Mingan continued. Running and shouting, the hunters rounded up the buffalo into stone-lined "pens" near the edge of cliffs. These pens were shaped like the letter *V*—wide at one end, but narrow near the edge of the cliff.

As the massive animals stampeded into the pen, the braves risked being trampled under their sharp hooves, but they wouldn't give up, driving the buffalo deeper into the pen and over the cliff. Then the Blackfoot braves had to climb down the cliff and carry the buffalo meat and skins back to camp.

AUSTRALIA HAS MORE THAN 400,000 FERAL HORSES, THE LARGEST POPULATION IN THE WORLD.

Male mustangs fight for mates. Their fights can be very violent but are over in just a few moments.

The chief ended his tales that night with a story about a noble brave who had given up his favorite buffalo horse so a younger man could ride her in his first hunt. When Chief Mingan finished his tale, he looked right at Chogan. The wise old chief had known all along why Apisi had given up Koko.

THE MUSTANG REVOLUTION

Mustangs changed the lives and culture of the Blackfoot and of all Native people. Because the horses made braves such as Chogan and Apisi more successful at chasing down buffalo, it took less time for them to provide food for their tribes. Now they had time to share the stories of their ancestors, make new tools, and create artwork.

With domesticated mustangs the Blackfoot could cover as much as 80 kilometers (50 miles) in a day. Children and old people no longer slowed down the tribe as it migrated. The elders sat on the horses' backs, while the babies were tied

to the saddles. Tribes made more contact with one another. They traded objects, exchanged ideas—and often fought. Horses made warfare faster and more vicious than when the braves had fought on foot.

Before horses, when Native people followed the migrating buffalo herds, they relied on dogs to transport their possessions. The Blackfoot would load packs on a *travois*, a kind of sled made up of two long poles. Horses could pull a lot more weight, and so the Blackfoot accumulated more possessions. Women crafted beautiful bridles, saddles, and other crafts to show off the beauty of their horses and tell the story of their people.

And there could be a lot for the horses to haul: food, tools, weapons, clothing. As well, the tepees had to be

Many tribes across North America used horse-drawn travois *to transport their belongings.*

IF YOU HEAR A HORSE BLOW SOFTLY THROUGH ITS NOSE, IT'S CURIOUS OR RELAXED.

Sable Island Ponies

Off the coast of Nova Scotia, on Canada's Atlantic Ocean shore, lies a windswept little island. Sable Island is famous for being home to a group of small hardy ponies.

At one point historians thought the horses swam to Sable Island hundreds of years ago, after one of the area's many shipwrecks. Now they believe settlers left them there in the 1700s.

Life on Sable Island is difficult for the tiny, stocky ponies. There's not much shelter from the wind and blowing sand. In winter, it's hard for the horses to find grass to eat. Luckily, the animals seem to have a special sense for where to dig to find a drink. There is sand in everything they eat, which wears down their teeth and makes it hard for the ponies to grind the tough grasses.

Today, up to 400 horses live on Sable Island. To protect the animals and make sure they remain wild, only about 50 people are allowed to visit the island each year. Most of them are scientists, and they must have permission from the Canadian Coast Guard.

North America has other island horses that live free. The Chincoteague Pony, also known as the Assateague horse, lives on Assateague Island, off the coast of Virginia and Maryland.

moved, and every one was made of 12 to 14 buffalo hides, each weighing about 4.5 kilograms (10 pounds). (Some enormous tepees needed as many as 40 skins!) The long, heavy poles—as many as 20—that formed the frame of each tepee were transported, too. In fact, they were often used to form the frame of the *travois*.

WESTERN ICON

The Blackfoot and other tribes no longer hunt buffalo, but are still known for their skill with horses. However, the Native people didn't domesticate all the mustangs, and many of the horses continued to wander freely across the Great Plain, a vast area that stretched between the Mississippi River in the east and the Rocky Mountains in the west. There, they found plenty to eat. The grasses swayed in the breeze like a boundless green ocean and cold streams provided crystal-clear water to drink.

The mustangs typically lived in large herds led by an experienced old mare who kept them safe and well fed. To survive and stay safe from predators, the mustangs developed sharp vision, a keen sense of smell, and excellent hearing.

About a hundred years ago, there were 2 million mustangs in North America. As cattle ranches took over more land, there was less rangeland for the mustangs and their numbers plummeted. So, in 1979, the horses were designated an endangered species. The population of mustangs began to grow again and now there are about 35,000 roaming free. Today, mustangs are symbols of freedom, the strength of Native courage, and the spirit of North America's West.

"Holy Dogs"

The Blackfoot were just one of the many Native American tribes that depended on mustangs. Lakota called them *shunka wakan* or "holy dogs," since their speed made them seem supernatural. The Crow people were renowned for the quality of their horses, while the Comanche and Cheyenne were famous as skilled riders.

Most tribes had a favorite horse color. For instance, the Sioux preferred chestnut horses—they have a light reddish-brown coat, mane, and tail. Another popular coat color among Native peoples was pinto: large patches of white along with another color.

WILD PONIES FROM CHINCOTEAGUE ARE ALSO PAINTERS— YOU CAN SEE THEIR WORK ONLINE.

Patriotic Horse

Star, Unsung Hero of the Revolutionary War

What was that? Sybil swiftly turned her horse, Star, off the trail into a dense thicket.

Someone was coming down the path, right toward them! Sybil held her breath. *Please keep still, Star,* she thought.

A moment later, two rough-looking men crept stealthily down the trail. Spying through the branches, Sybil saw them and shuddered. Were they enemy soldiers or thieves? It hardly mattered—either group would kill a young woman like her. Laying her hand on Star's strong neck reassured Sybil a little.

"I told thee, I heard something," one of the men hissed to the other.

"No one is out on a wet night like tonight," replied the second man angrily. "Thou art hearing things again. Let's go warm up with a pint of ale."

Sybil watched the men disappear, then anxiously waited a few more moments to make sure they didn't return. Sighing with relief, she finally wheeled Star back onto the path.

"Good old Star," Sybil whispered, patting her horse. "Thee didn't make a sound. Now run fast—the Patriots are depending on us!"

A KNOCK AT THE DOOR

BANG! BANG! BANG!

Colonel Henry Ludington and his family stared at the front door and then at each other. The low glow from the fire on the hearth showed the fear in their eyes. Who could be knocking at nine o'clock on a dark, wet April night?

In Connecticut in 1777, you couldn't always trust your neighbors. The American Revolution had begun just two years earlier, and Henry knew the British enemy had put a price on his head because he was such a brave leader for the American side. Perhaps a British spy in the community had passed along word that Henry was at home that night with only his family. Were enemy troops at the door, waiting to take him away?

Trouble had been brewing between the British and the Americans for years before the Revolutionary War began. The British government made new laws for the colonies and demanded higher taxes, but the United States had no say in electing the British government or in what laws were enacted. Thirteen of the colonies (known as states today) decided to rebel. The settlers boycotted the things they'd been buying from English traders. In Boston Harbor in 1773, one group threw the tea on an English ship overboard—an incident that became famous as the Boston Tea Party.

Sybil Ludington

Today, no one knows for sure what Sybil or Star looked like. But there's no doubt they were both strong and brave.

On April 19, 1775, the war officially began with battles in the Massachusetts towns of Lexington and Concord, about 300 kilometers (185 miles) from where the Ludingtons lived. On July 4, 1776, the group governing the thirteen colonies signed the Declaration of Independence, stating that they were forming a new nation called the United States of America.

The war raged on, with many deaths and injuries on both sides. On April 25, 1777, about 2,000 British soldiers arrived by warship at Fairfield, Connecticut, and began marching inland. The next day they moved into Danbury, a town just 27 kilometers (17 miles) from the Ludington farmhouse.

DANBURY IN DANGER

On that icy, stormy April night long ago, Henry Ludington cautiously opened the door and a soaking wet, exhausted man almost fell into the room. He had ridden his horse from Danbury to deliver the latest news—and it wasn't good.

Panting for breath, the messenger gasped out a terrible report of how the British were burning Danbury and all the Patriot supplies stored there. A spy had told the British about the supply depot, and since the Patriots thought it was secret, it wasn't heavily guarded. Meat, corn, and flour to feed American troops, as well as tents, clothes, and shoes were all gone.

Henry quickly realized he would have to gather his troops to fight the British. But his soldiers were scattered over the countryside. They were ordinary citizens who'd been given permission to return to their farms. These non-professional soldiers, known as militia, had to

When the militiamen were given time away from battle to plant their crops, they made sure they kept their guns close by for protection.

take time away from military duties to get their crops planted or there'd be no food for their families next winter.

The men deserved and needed the break, but Henry had no choice. He gave orders to the messenger to continue riding through the countryside, summoning the militia to muster at the Ludington farm and prepare for battle. Immediately.

But the messenger just stared at Henry wearily.

BRAVE RIDER NEEDED

The rider was far too cold, wet, and exhausted to go back out into the rainy night. He also didn't know the territory. But who else could go? Not Henry—he needed to stay at the farm to organize the soldiers when they arrived. His wife was busy putting the youngest of their many children

This ancient pottery horse shows the horse collar invented in China.

to bed and didn't know where all the militiamen's farms were anyway.

But there *was* someone—someone who not only knew the neighborhood well, but also knew who was in her father's militia and where all the men lived: Henry's oldest child, 16-year-old Sybil. She helped out at home with sewing, candle-making, gardening, and all the other domestic tasks that a properly brought-up young lady in the late 1700s needed to know. Whenever Sybil had time, however, she loved to sneak outside to watch her father drill his men to improve their shooting and marching. (Since most of them couldn't afford horses, they marched into battle rather than riding on horseback.)

Not only did Sybil know all the men in the militia and where they lived, she was also a good horseback rider, with a strong, fast horse named Star. So, on the stormy night of April 26, 1777, Sybil and Star started out on their history-making ride.

THE RIDE BEGINS

Back in the late 1700s, 16-year-olds were considered adults. After all, Sybil's mother wasn't even 15 when she married Sybil's father. But Henry knew that the journey ahead of his daughter would be difficult for even the most experienced riders. On this wild night, she would have to ride 64 kilometers (40 miles) on mostly unmarked trails that were slippery with rain and mud.

Henry must have watched his daughter go with a heavy heart. How could Star gallop over such slick, muddy tracks? Would Sybil ever make it home again?

"MUSTER AT LUDINGTON'S!"

Sybil headed out of the farmhouse gate, and toward the first soldier's farmhouse. The icy rain stung her eyes and it wasn't long before her shawl was soaked through. Star's warm body gave her some comfort as the pair raced down the road. The wind whipped around them and mud splashed under Star's flying hooves. The reins were slippery but Sybil hung on and turned into the first farmyard.

Star bolted up to the door and Sybil banged on it with the stick she carried—thanks to the stick, she didn't have to take time to dismount. What a relief when a window finally opened and a tired farmer stuck his head out to see who was making such a ruckus! Sybil quickly gasped out the news of the Danbury attack and Colonel Ludington's order to muster at his farm. The soldier had often seen Sybil there so he knew he could trust that the message was official.

Sybil hardly had time to catch her breath before she and Star were swinging around and sprinting to the next farm. The rain pelted down, making it hard to see through the murky night.

"Muster at Ludington's," she yelled at each farmhouse, waiting barely long enough for a shutter to open or a sleepy head to poke out a window before she and Star dashed off again. The farms were scattered over the countryside, with long distances between them, and her father was counting on Sybil to get to them all.

A HORSE'S MANE AND ITS FORE-LOCK (THE HAIR BETWEEN THE EARS) DIRECT RAIN DOWN OFF THE ANIMAL, HELPING THE HORSE TO STAY A LITTLE DRIER.

In the early 1900s, sheriffs on horse-back in the North American west could quietly track criminals and take them by surprise.

Stop That Horse!

Not everyone used horses for patriotic or honest work. Criminals on horseback held up trains, and cattle thieves rode horses when stealing livestock.

The most famous thieves on horseback were highwaymen, who robbed travelers in England from the late 1500s to the early 1800s. In America they were called road agents, while in Australia they were known as bushrangers. Their famous demand, "Stand and deliver!" meant "Hand over all your money!" Refusal might mean death.

Sheriffs and police pursued these criminals on horseback, and doctors rode horses to reach the victims of these criminals so they could patch them up.

TREACHEROUS TRAILS

On through the night Sybil and Star sped over the country-side. The rough roads Star had to run on were rutted and uneven. But Sybil also had to ride down narrow trails through thick swamps and woods. These woods were dangerous because they were often full of British soldiers—and worse. Lurking on the forest paths were criminals called "cowboys" who stole from anyone for the British army.

Even more menacing were men known as "skinners." They weren't loyal to either side and simply stole anything they could get their hands on and killed at random.

And, of course, Sybil also had to avoid any farms belonging to families still loyal to the British king. If any of them discovered that the local militia were gathering, they might get word to the British army.

As Sybil raced along, she may have thought of other times she had helped her father and the Patriot cause. Once, Sybil's father had proved to be such a good protector of the Americans' supplies that the British put out a big reward for his capture. It wasn't long before more than 50 armed men surrounded the Ludington house, planning to kidnap him.

But rumors had reached Sybil about the reward and she was keeping guard on the house, as she did many nights. One dark night she spotted men sneaking closer. She directed her brothers and sisters to light candles in the windows. Then they all grabbed sticks and muskets and marched past the windows as if they were on guard—the candlelight made their shadows large and easy to see from outside. It was impossible for the men to tell that they were only children, and not strong adult soldiers. The attackers were fooled into thinking the colonel was well guarded and they left empty-handed.

Sybil hoped she and Star would be able to help her father as much this night.

ALMOST HOME

The morning sun was just beginning to flush the eastern sky red as Sybil and Star wearily plodded down the last stretch of road toward home. They were cold and soaking wet and Sybil could barely keep her eyes open. Her skirts and petticoats were thick with mud. Star's hooves were caked with dirt and he was moving slowly.

The brave pair had ridden all night, hour after hour. But never once along those rough roads and slippery trails had Star faltered. He had carried Sybil through those perilous woods full of dangerous men.

Have Horse, Will Travel

In the late 1600s, horses provided the power for the first taxis in Paris. By the 1700s, people were traveling between European towns in regularly scheduled horse-drawn coaches.

People began to travel for fun. On a good road, a horse could move at about 37 kilometers (23 miles) per hour, or about as fast as a car on a slow city street. A horse-drawn coach could wheel along at about half that speed.

In 1819, horses pulled the first buses—they looked like large stagecoaches—in Paris. Horses even helped people travel by water by pulling barges along canals.

STAR MAY HAVE RECEIVED HIS NAME BECAUSE HE HAD A SMALL WHITE MARK, KNOWN AS A STAR, ON HIS FOREHEAD.

Sybil's throat ached from calling out to the militiamen and alerting her neighbors. But she had accomplished her task—she had mustered all of her father's troops. Sybil had done her best to help the Patriot cause. Soon she would know if the men had heeded her alarm or if they had decided to stay in their beds on this cold, wet night.

Sybil wiped the mud from her eyes, and patted Star's dirty, rain-soaked neck. Poor horse! Sybil had chosen to head out on this dangerous errand, but Star had had no choice. Still, he'd carried her safely this far. Soon, he would be in a warm stall and well fed. Sybil would make sure of that.

THE MILITIA HEAD OUT

When Sybil and Star turned onto the track into her family's farm, she grinned to see the hundreds of men who had left their homes to fight with her father for their country's future. The soldiers cheered when they spotted the brave girl and her horse.

Colonel Ludington and his men marched out soon after daybreak. They were too late to save Danbury, but they joined with other militia to fight the British at the Battle of Ridgefield on April 27, 1777, and caused many casualties on the British side. When General George Washington, the leader of the American troops and the future country's first president, heard of Sybil's incredible ride, he rode to her house to personally thank her for her service to the Patriot cause.

MANY PEOPLE THINK STAR WAS A BAY. THAT MEANS HIS COAT WAS REDDISH BROWN, WITH BLACK MANE, LEGS, AND TAIL. BAY IS THE MOST COMMON HORSE COLOR.

SYBIL REMEMBERED

The story of Sybil's brave ride was kept in her family until long after she died. When the tale was finally written down, some of the details were no longer very clear. Most people say Sybil's horse was named Star and that he was reddish brown, but there are no written records about him dating back to the time when he lived.

On March 25, 1975, Sybil and Star were pictured on a stamp that was part of an American Bicentennial series. Sybil was only the thirty-fifth woman honored with a United States postage stamp.

Everyone says that Sybil showed great courage, but that's about all they agree on. Some reports say Sybil carried a musket and dressed in men's clothes. Others say she carried a stick, which would definitely have been handy for knocking on doors or protecting herself from thieves or British soldiers.

Some stories say Sybil rode sidesaddle, which means she didn't straddle Star, but sat with both legs on one side. That's the way well-bred young ladies rode in those days. Women hadn't been allowed to ride at all until around 1200, when the sidesaddle was invented—many cultures had thought it was indecent for women to sit with a leg on either side of a horse. The sidesaddle was uncomfortable and unsafe, but was widely used from about 1300 to the early

IN MANY LANGUAGES, THE WORD FOR *HORSE* COMES FROM A TERM MEANING "TO HASTEN." HORSES SPED UP HOW FAST HUMANS MOVED THEMSELVES, FOOD, AND MORE.

1900s, when women were finally able to do many things that today are taken for granted—such as wear pants, vote, and hold jobs outside the home.

Today, it's hard to know for sure how Sybil sat on Star and rode through the night. Statues that honor Sybil stand in Carmel, New York, near where her ride took place, as well as in Washington, DC; Danbury, Connecticut; and Murrells Inlet, South Carolina: they all show her riding sidesaddle.

Sybil and Star were commemorated on a postage stamp in 1975. Towns near Ludingtonville celebrate Sybil Ludington Day around April 26 each year. There's even been an opera written about Sybil's ride, called *Sybil, Daughter of the American Revolution*, by Ludmila Ulehla. Fredericksburg, where Sybil lived, was renamed Ludingtonville in honor of her family. Road signs mark the route she and Star are believed to have taken on that fateful night.

THE WAR ENDS

Sybil's ride on April 26, 1777, changed history, and she couldn't have done it without Star. Without a horse to ride, Sybil would not have been able to muster her father's troops in time to fight the British. Although the British burned Danbury and won the Battle of Ridgefield, anger at the destruction caused by the British and pride in acts such as Sybil's brave ride motivated the Americans. Never again during the rest of the war would British troops be able to raid as far into the Connecticut countryside.

The Americans went on to win the war in 1783 and create a new, free country, independent of Britain. The American Revolutionary War shows what happens when ordinary people—including a brave girl on horseback—are willing to risk everything to protect their liberty.

CHANGING THE WORLD ON HORSEBACK

When Sybil made her historic ride, there were no trains, cars, or planes. Riding a horse was the quickest way to travel.

People have been riding horses since about 3500 BCE. Before that, people used horses for carrying packs or pulling loads on sleds. But one day, someone on the grasslands of southern Russia or west-central Asia may have climbed up on his horse to adjust a bundle, or to try to see a little farther over a grassy plain. No one knows how someone first thought of riding a horse, but people soon realized how much faster it was than walking.

From about 1700 to 1900 CE, horseback was the most popular way for people to travel or move their goods. Farmers used horses to transport their vegetables and grain, which connected villages and increased trade and wealth, since the farmers could sell to more people. Horses also pulled carts of timber and stones to early towns, providing more supplies for the builders and carpenters and allowing them to create the larger, more elaborate cities still admired today.

Actors, musicians, and other performers traveled by horse to reach new audiences. Horses allowed traveling salesmen, schoolmasters, and religious leaders to visit isolated farmhouses. This helped spread education and new ideas, changing how people thought.

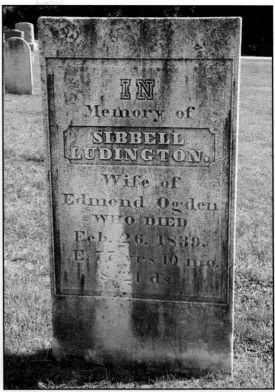

Her name is spelled "Sibbell" on her gravestone, although today most people know her as Sybil Ludington.

THE MOST POPULAR NAMES FOR HORSES ARE SHORT—LIKE STAR—PROBABLY BECAUSE MOST HORSES CAN BE TAUGHT TO RECOGNIZE SHORT WORDS AND THEIR MEANINGS.

The stagecoach got its name because it made regular trips between stations, or stages, which were places where travelers could take a break.

Cars and other machinery have now replaced horses in many parts of world; however, millions of horses, donkeys, and mules continue to be used for transportation in many countries, including Afghanistan, Morocco, and Paraguay.

Horses still transport people in wilderness areas, where even jeeps can't go or where heavy vehicles would harm delicate soil and plants or small animals. Horses are also used in nature reserves because they're quieter than motorized vehicles. Some park rangers and game wardens ride horses on patrol.

From the first riders who lived thousands of years ago to brave Patriots like Sybil Ludington and right up to today, horses have carried people and changed the world, one step at a time.

The Pony Express

Cross-Country Mail Movers

The wolves' howls were coming closer now. Jack shivered. He knew a wolf could badly maul his horse—and him!

This part of the trail wasn't too dangerous by daylight. But the last Pony Express rider had been delayed by a snowstorm, which meant Jack was two hours late leaving his station.

Dusk was falling and the wolves were boldly out to chase their dinner. *But they won't be dinin' on Lightning or me,* thought Jack. *Not if I can help it!*

"C'mon, Lightning, c'mon!"

Jack braved a quick look over his shoulder. He could see low, dark shapes loping up the trail behind him. How many wolves were chasing them? Five? Six? Jack quickly turned back around. "Run, Lightning, run," he yelled.

Jack saw a flickering light in the distance. The next Pony Express station was just ahead!

"Lightning, we're almost there—we're gonna make it!"

DELAYED DELIVERY

When gold was discovered in California on January 24, 1848, one of the world's biggest gold rushes began, and within two years, nearly 300,000 people from all across America (and the world) rushed to seek their fortunes. Far from home, they wanted mail from their families, as well as news from the rest of the country.

But it seemed as if mail took forever to arrive in California. Ships from the east coast of the United States had to sail down around the tip of South America, then back up the west coast, which could take six months.

By 1857, stagecoaches could carry the mail from St. Louis, Missouri, to San Francisco, California, in about 25 days. But that just wasn't fast enough. What about a relay system of horses and riders to move mail quickly across the country?

The time had come for the Pony Express to gallop into American history.

Pony Express riders and their horses often faced fierce snow-storms in the mountains.

RIDERS HAD TO WEIGH LESS THAN 57 KILOGRAMS (125 POUNDS).

THE RIDE BEGINS

"Go, James, go," cheered the crowd outside the Alta Telegraph Office in San Francisco on April 3, 1860. A buff-colored pony pranced with excitement, just waiting for his rider to leap aboard.

Galloping Through History

But before Pony Express rider James Randall could begin his historic ride, there was one thing left to do. He slung the leather *mochila* (pronounced *moe-CHEE-la*) over his saddle. *Mochila* is a Spanish word that means "backpack," and it held the mail that James would be carrying on the first leg of its trip. The bag was designed to be slung on and off the saddle in a hurry. On each corner of the *mochila* was a locked pouch, called a *cantina* (kan-TEE-nuh), to hold the mail.

Once the *mochila* was in place, James mounted his horse and raced through the crowd to the waterfront. He didn't have far to go—just to the deck of the steamboat *Antelope*.

THROUGH THE WET, DARK NIGHT

The *Antelope* arrived late that rainy night in Sacramento, California, and that was when the Pony Express really began its incredible eastward journey. Rider Billy Hamilton waited at the dock, his horse ready to gallop away. The young man grabbed the *mochila*, leapt onto his horse's back, and headed off into the wet, inky darkness.

The ride had barely begun and already Billy was worried. He was used to rain and slick roads so he wasn't concerned for himself. But he was sure that rain in Sacramento meant snow in the mountains for the Pony Express rider who would take the *mochila* from him. At this time of year, snowstorms were fierce and dangerous, and certain to slow down any riders out in them.

Billy knew another group of Pony Express riders would be heading west with mail at the same time as he and the western riders were heading east. There was no way he was going to let those westbound riders complete their ride faster than he and his companion! So Billy rode his horse as quickly as he could through the storm and darkness, hoping

Ride On!

Pony Express riders had to be small, to cut down on the weight the horse had to carry, and tough. They faced death every day and spent many long, lonely hours in wild territory with just their horse for a companion.

Sometimes a rider would pull up to a station, just aching to get out of the saddle, have a meal, and rest. But if there was no new rider there to keep the mail moving, the exhausted rider would have to grab his *mochila*, jump on a fresh horse, and keep going.

ONLY ONE MAIL SHIPMENT WAS EVER LOST DURING THE RUNNING OF THE PONY EXPRESS.

THE PONY EXPRESS ADVERTISED IT COULD DELIVER MAIL IN 10 DAYS, BUT IN WINTER IT COULD TAKE 16.

to gain some time to balance out the delay sure to hamper the next rider.

Billy rode all night, quickly switching horses five times at Pony Express stations, then thundering off into the night on a fresh horse. The brave young rider covered almost 100 kilometers (60 miles). He was exhausted, but early in the morning, when he handed over the *mochila* to the next rider, Warren Upson, the Pony Express was half an hour ahead of schedule.

Warren was mighty grateful. He knew that he'd need the extra half hour to stay on schedule. His portion of the Pony Express trail would be the most grueling of the entire route.

Pony Express Route: April 3, 1880 – October 24, 1881

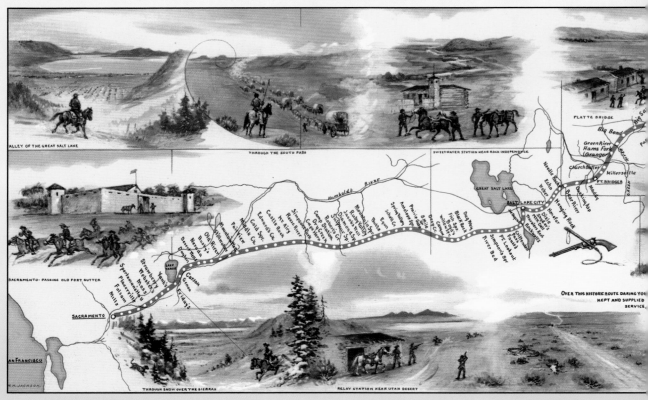

CALIFORNIA **NEVADA** **UTAH** **WYOMING**

THE STORMY SIERRA NEVADA

As he headed up into the Sierra Nevada mountain range, Warren's heart sank—there was a lot of snow here, with more swirling down. It was so deep that at times Warren had to dismount and lead his horse. The trail was steep and precarious, and icy winds blew around the rider and his mount. His horse had to be especially sure-footed since canyons fell away on either side of the trail. The freezing, trembling animal picked its way carefully.

The snow blinded Warren and stung his face, but he just kept climbing upward. When he finally had a sense that he was heading downhill, he knew he'd managed to cross the pass.

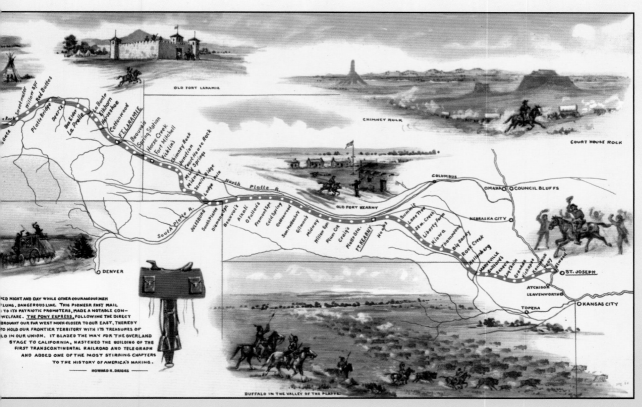

COLORADO   NEBRASKA   KANSAS   MISSOURI

THE PONY EXPRESS

Conditions began to improve as Warren and his horse wound their way down the mountains. He was relieved to finally pass the *mochila* to the next rider and collapse. But the Pony Express mail wasn't safe yet.

FLOOD!

All was almost lost when the next rider tried to cross the Platte River in Nebraska. Rain had flooded the riverbanks and the Pony Express horse was swept away by the current. The waiting crowd screamed in horror as the rider scrambled off—making sure to grab the mail first! One of the towns-people gave him a fresh horse, though, and the rider continued on his way while his brave horse was rescued from the rushing river.

The horses galloped on, through scorching wastelands and lowland swamps full of mosquitoes. In buffalo country, the big, shaggy beasts hardly looked up from their grazing as the horse galloped by. Rattlesnakes waited on the desert trails, but the Pony Express riders resolutely kept going.

MEANWHILE, BACK IN MISSOURI . . .

On April 3, 1860, the same day the Pony Express mail headed east from San Francisco, Johnny Fry was waiting impatiently in St. Joseph, Missouri, to carry the mail west. He should have started hours before James Randall began his ride in California. But the train bringing the mail from farther east was late, and Johnny couldn't begin his historic ride without the mail.

Johnny's little bay mare stamped her feet nervously. She seemed as impatient as Johnny! Finally, the crowd gathered around Johnny heard the train approaching. It pulled into town, and a cannon boomed as the townspeople cheered.

Home Away from Home

There were two different types of stations on the Pony Express trail. At the relay stations the riders switched horses. These stations were about 16 kilometers (10 miles) apart, or the distance a horse could gallop before tiring. Relay stations changed locations during the Pony Express, and there were between 88 and 159 of them.

The home stations were about 120 kilometers (75 miles) apart and were often located in forts or stagecoach stations. Here, riders could eat and sleep while waiting for a rider to arrive bringing the mail in the opposite direction.

THERE WERE 25 HOME STATIONS ON THE PONY EXPRESS TRAIL.

With the *mochila* full of mail—including a telegram of congratulations on the Pony Express's first run from United States president James Buchanan to the governor of California—Johnny and his horse thundered down to the waterfront and onto the ferry that would carry them across the Missouri River and into Kansas.

Just like James on the west coast, Johnny was determined to move the mail as fast as he could. He wanted to make up some of the time he had lost waiting for the late train. So when he galloped into each station to change to a fresh horse, he flipped the *mochila* from one saddle to the next in seconds instead of minutes. Late that night, when he handed the *mochila* over to Don Rising, the next rider, Johnny had made up 45 minutes of the lost time. As Don headed off into the night, Johnny gulped down a quick meal of beans and bacon and slumped exhausted onto the station's bed.

NO TIME TO REST

The Pony Express riders kept the mail moving across the lonely plains and treacherous mountain trails. At each station, the rider would fling himself and the *mochila* onto a fresh horse, then gallop about 20 kilometers (12 miles) to the next station. There he would rest until the mail heading in the opposite direction arrived at the station. On Sunday, April 8, the eastbound rider and the westbound rider passed each other just east of Salt Lake City, Utah.

Now all the riders would retrace the trails they'd ridden only days before, but this time with their *mochila*s filled with new batches of mail. On April 13, bells clanged and crowds roared as an exhausted

Morgan horses are known for having intelligence, strength, a good disposition, and courage.

Pony Express Breeds

Pony Express breeds included Morgans (a versatile breed and one of the first developed in the United States) and Thoroughbreds (a spirited, speedy breed), which were often used on the eastern end of the trail.

In the middle of the route, the Express riders rode pintos—*pinto* is a Spanish word meaning "painted" or "spotted." Mustangs (page 13) were often used for the western (more rugged) part of the mail route.

Today the United States has more pinto horses than any other country in the world.

Buffalo Bill

Probably the most famous Pony Express rider was William "Buffalo Bill" Cody. Today, historians aren't sure he actually ever rode for the Pony Express, but he kept the memory of riders and their horses alive with his Wild West show.

Featuring famous sharpshooter Annie Oakley and storyteller Calamity Jane, the show included reenactments of the Pony Express, stagecoach robberies, and more. Buffalo Bill toured North America and Europe with his show, performing for huge crowds that often included royalty.

46

Billy Hamilton rode back into Sacramento and down to the dock where the boat was waiting to carry the mail to San Francisco.

On that same night, Johnny Fry and his horse were again sailing across the Missouri River, but this time they were heading east toward St. Joseph. Glittering fireworks and thick gunsmoke filled the air as people celebrated the success and speed of the Pony Express. The Pony Express riders had carried the mail 3,164 kilometers (1,966 miles) from California to Missouri in 10 days, or less than half the time it would take by stagecoach.

But there was no time to rest. After a short break, the riders and horses were back on the trail, making another Pony Express delivery.

Buffalo Bill is said to have held the record for the longest Pony Express ride. He rode 21 horses to travel 518 kilometers (322 miles) non-stop.

SPECIAL DELIVERY

In November 1860, westbound horses brought perhaps the most important news the Pony Express ever carried: the results of the country's presidential election. The newspapers had been specially printed on lightweight paper to reduce the cost of delivery, since it was calculated by weight. The papers were wrapped in oiled, waterproof silk to keep them dry even if the riders had to press on through snowstorms or raging rivers. Soon the news reached San Francisco: Abraham Lincoln was president.

Against incredible odds, Pony Express riders carried the text of Lincoln's first speech as president

A Handy Measurement

Did you know a horse's height isn't measured to the top of its head? That's because the head height can change a lot, depending on how the horse is standing. Instead, a horse's height is measured from the ground to the top of its shoulders (withers).

There's also a special unit for measuring how tall a horse is. It's called a "hand," and it's 10 centimeters (4 inches) high. Long ago, people didn't carry measuring tapes. If someone needed to quickly measure a horse, he used a unit he always had with him: the width of his hand.

across the country in less than eight days. That was the fastest run ever. Americans wondered if their country was on the brink of war (northern states and southern states disagreed on many issues). Lincoln tried to keep the peace between the North and the South, but in April the Civil War broke out. Pony Express horses carried this news, too.

However, the days of the Pony Express were numbered. Crews running wires to carry telegraph messages across America were hard at work. One group began on the west coast while another started on the east. On October 24, 1861, the two groups met in Salt Lake City, Utah. The country was now connected by wire from coast to coast and messages could be sent electrically in seconds. Suddenly, the tough little Pony Express horses and their riders were too slow.

Team Pony vs. Team Horse

It was called the Pony Express but most of the riders rode horses. What's the difference between the two?

Horses tend to be bigger than ponies, standing at least 14.2 hands, or 145 centimeters (57 inches). A pony not only has shorter legs than a horse, it also has a thicker neck, wider trunk (or barrel), and its head is shorter with a broader forehead. Ponies usually have thicker coats, manes, and tails than horses and are calmer as well.

The last official run of a Pony Express rider took place on November 20, 1861.

MAIL ON THE HOOF

Even the experts no longer know for sure who sent the first message by horse, but it may have been Cyrus the Great, a Persian king. About 2,600 years ago, he set up a postal system to send messages across his vast kingdom. Like the Pony Express, Cyrus's service used fast horses and riders who rode in relay from one station to the next.

The Roman government copied Cyrus's system a few centuries later, using light carriages pulled by fast horses. But the system fell apart as roads decayed and relay stations shut down when the Roman Empire crumbled. Horses were still carrying mail across Asia, but in Europe there was no reliable way to send a message from about 500 CE until the late 1700s. Messengers delivered the mail whenever they felt like it. Some message writers who wanted better service tried writing things like, *Ride, villain, ride for your life!* on their letters—but their notes still didn't move any faster.

That changed on August 2, 1874, when four horses pulled the first mail coach out of London, England. People feared passengers' health might be damaged because the coach rolled along so quickly: as fast as 18 kilometers (11 miles) per hour!

Around the world, telegraphs and faster delivery systems, such as by train and airplane, meant that horses were no longer used to move parcels and other mail. But even today, the postal service isn't completely

Frank E. Webner was one of the many brave, young, Pony Express riders.

On the Warpath

Weather and rough trails weren't the Pony Express riders' only problems. In May 1860, the Paiute Native people were starving and furious. Native people had negotiated treaties with the American government, but those treaties were being broken. As well, settlers were killing buffalo in huge numbers and Native people depended on those animals for food.

The Paiute began attacking Pony Express riders and stations. For more than 20 days, the delivery system was at a standstill with the mail going nowhere. A Paiute chief helped restore some order but raids on the Pony Express riders and stations continued.

Pony Express routes were often lonely; riders probably welcomed the company of workers erecting telegraph poles and wires. But the telegraph soon put the Pony Express rider out of work.

finished with horses—mules (a relation of horses; see page 55) still carry mail in and out of two locations deep in the Grand Canyon.

UNITED BY HORSES

Despite operating for only 18 months, the Pony Express is one of the best-known chapters in American history. Its tough, strong horses carried almost 35,000 pieces of mail and galloped more than 965,600 kilometers (600,000 miles). The fast service changed people's expectations of how quickly they should receive political and social news.

About 180 young men had ridden the difficult trails on their brave horses and faced the many dangers. In 1869, railways would link the American east coast with the west, but the Pony Express had helped keep the country united through the dark days leading up to the American Civil War.

The Pony Express Rides Again

Every June, the National Pony Express Association (NPEA) stages a reenactment of a Pony Express ride. Each rider covers up to 16 kilometers (10 miles) and must be able to change horses and *mochilas* in less than 15 minutes.

In May 1996, NPEA riders carried the Olympic torch during the torch relay leading up to the Olympic Games in Atlanta, Georgia.

Galloping Through History

Pit Ponies

Fueling Industry from Deep Underground

The pony held his ground. No matter what Harry did, no matter how hard he pulled on the little animal's reins, he couldn't budge the pony and his cart full of coal.

"C'mon, Blackie," coaxed the miner. "It's perfectly safe, it's—"

Suddenly, Harry heard a low rumble. A cave-in just ahead! "Turn around, Blackie! Turn around now. We've got to get out of here!"

This time, the little Shetland pony needed no urging. He spun around so quickly, he spilled some of the coal from his cart. "Let's go," yelled Harry, racing along beside his pony. The pair dashed through the dimly lit tunnel.

"Good ol' Blackie," Harry gasped as he ran. "You knew about the cave-in before I did! I reckon you saved my life again. There's an apple waiting for you when we reach the main shaft!"

HORSES FAR BELOW

When the Industrial Revolution hit Europe in the late 1700s, it changed the world for people—and for horses. Machines now did jobs (such as weaving cloth and making tools) that had once been done by hand. Suddenly, factories and workshops were being powered by steam engines, and steam engines needed lots of coal.

Life especially changed in England, where much of the population went to work in the coal mines. Men dug the coal and women lugged it out of the mines. But in 1842, the British government decided this work was too difficult and dangerous for women, and outlawed them from working in the mines. Now who would carry the coal out?

Horses were lowered into (and raised out of) a mine using a cage and a winch, which is a mechanical device that lengthens or shortens a cable.

For thousands of years, horses had been busy pulling wagons and carrying people—aboveground. But some of those horses, and especially ponies, now headed down into the mines to haul carts full of coal.

INTO THE MINE

Blackie wasn't born in the mines but he was still just a young pony when he and the other Shetlands on the Thomsons' farm were first walked to the coal mine. One by one the

Galloping Through History

other ponies were fastened into a cage and lowered into the ground.

Then it was Blackie's turn. He whinnied with fear and bucked and kicked, but the men spoke softly and kindly to him as they carefully tied him in place so he couldn't thrash around and hurt himself. A winch dropped the cage deep into the mine. Blackie must have been scared as he dangled in the air before falling, down, down, down the shaft.

There was no bright, warming sun at the bottom, but thanks to the lamps hanging on the walls, Blackie would have been able to see the other ponies. More men unfastened his ties and led him to a cozy, clean stable, where there were even more ponies, some of whom were older and had already been working in the mine for many years.

UNDERGROUND STABLES

The stables were surprisingly comfortable, with high ceilings. They had good drainage and were also well ventilated, with fans carefully placed so they wouldn't blow directly on the ponies.

But there was one way the stables were different from the ones Blackie had been used to aboveground. These stalls were built using as little wood as possible so there would be nothing to fuel a fire. Miners were very careful to avoid the chance of a spark igniting a fire deep underground or causing an explosion due to gases and dust in the thick air. That was why the ponies slept on sawdust or peat (not on straw, like horses outside the mines). Luckily, these materials still kept them comfortable.

Blackie nickered loudly whenever he heard Tim, a groomsman, coming into the stables. The little pony had learned quickly that Tim's arrival meant he was about to be

Pit Ponies Around the World

Horses and ponies were used in coal mines not just in England but in countries around the world, including Australia and Germany. The mines in Belgium and France also used larger draft horses, such as Percherons, Friesians, and Belgians.

In the United States, the Appalachia coal fields in Kentucky and Pennsylvania used donkeys as well as ponies. Pit ponies also worked hard in the coal mines of Cape Breton Island, Nova Scotia, on Canada's east coast.

HORSES IN MINES WORE BRASS SHOES BECAUSE THIS METAL DOESN'T CAUSE DANGEROUS SPARKS THE WAY OTHER METALS CAN.

fed or get fresh water. The mine owners had realized that their ponies performed better if they were fed, groomed, and cared for by just one groomsman. So every day, Tim took care of Blackie, as well as Pip, Catherine, Glitter, and Wallace. In fact, Tim took care of Blackie throughout the pony's entire career in the pit.

Mine owners knew how vital ponies like Blackie were to the operation of the mine and its profits, so they took good care of the animals. Veterinarians frequently examined all the ponies to make sure they were healthy and that their legs were strong.

Even above ground, this pit pony is wearing a face covering to protect its eyes. Find out more about eye shields on page 56.

Galloping Through History

A REAL WORKING PONY

Blackie wasn't allowed to work until he was about four years old—that was the law. So he spent his days training for when he would become a real pit pony. Tim taught him how to wear a bridle, pull a cart, obey hand signals and voice commands, and much more. Life in the mines could be dangerous, what with rockslides and gas leaks, and Blackie had to learn to keep himself and the miners safe.

The little pony also had to grow until he was strong enough to pull a mine cart—some held as much as one or two tons of coal. Like Blackie, the best pit ponies were full-bodied, large-boned, and hearty. Pit ponies also had to be sure-footed since the underground tunnels were rough and steep.

Finally the day came when Blackie went to work! Now he spent every day with a driver named Harry, standing still while workers shoveled coal into his cart. Blackie must have noticed how low the ceilings were in the passages. It was because of those low tunnels that the mines used ponies and not full-sized horses.

Good-tempered and obedient, Blackie made an excellent pit pony. Timid ponies could be too expensive and time-consuming to train. Nervous ponies, like one of Blackie's stable mates named Mouse, were taken out of the mine, never to return. Major, a vicious pony, was also taken away. Major had nipped Blackie once with his sharp teeth, and Blackie had learned to keep his distance. Mean animals were a menace underground. They could hurt miners—or other ponies—and cause deadly accidents.

If the Shoe Fits

The rocky tunnels were tough on the pit ponies' feet, so they wore horseshoes, which were checked daily to make sure they were in good condition. A horseshoe maker, called a farrier (pronounced *FAIR-ee-er*), descended into the mine to measure the ponies' feet, then returned to the surface to make the shoes. The farrier couldn't make the shoes in the mine because the hot fire he needed to bend the metal would be too dangerous deep underground.

Donkeys, Burros, and Mules

Similar to horses and ponies, but with longer, thicker ears, donkeys have been a working animal for at least 5,000 years. They were likely first domesticated in Egypt. Today, there are at least 41 million in the world. A small donkey is called a *burro*, the Spanish and Portuguese word for donkey.

Mate a male donkey with a female horse and the baby will be a mule. These animals are stronger than similar-sized horses, but tend to require less food.

The Power of a Horse

You probably know the term *horsepower*, but have you ever wondered what it has to do with horses? The word was first used in the late 1700s by Scottish engineer James Watt, who is famous for improving the steam engine.

Horsepower is a measurement of engine power, and Watt created it to describe the work his engine could do in terms people understood. He expressed the power of his steam engine in relation to how much coal a horse could lift. The engine in an average car today is about 125 to 200 horsepower.

The pit pony and his master worked an eight-hour shift. Harry took good care of Blackie, giving him an extra pat on the neck when he'd worked hard or slipping Blackie a treat when he had to stand still, waiting, for a long time. Like all the miners, Harry helped maintain the underground roadways and tunnels to prevent accidents. He brushed the ceilings to remove any rocks that might hurt Blackie's head.

Harry also made sure Blackie's horseshoes were in good shape. Shoes weren't the only "uniform" Blackie wore. A leather shield over his face protected his eyes: Harry didn't want his Blackie to lose an eye from flying rocks or protruding equipment, as many ponies did. Blackie also wore ear hoods so he wouldn't receive electrical shocks from low-hanging wires.

By the end of the day, Harry thought Blackie seemed happy to head back to the stables and relax. This was when he must have really appreciated the high

A pit pony had to keep its head low as it pulled heavy loads through the dark tunnels of a coal mine.

ceilings there. Since he'd worked all day with his head held low pulling the cart, at night he would be relieved to finally lift his head and relax his neck muscles.

MINING PARTNERS

Blackie worked hard, but some days he was full of mischief. Like the time he decided he'd pulled enough for awhile and just sat down on the job. Harry and two other drivers couldn't budge him, so work stopped until Blackie decided his break was over. Another day, a pony named Bumble faked a limp until he'd hobbled back to the comfort of his stables, where he miraculously recovered.

Harry often shared his lunch with Blackie, and the driver's wife sometimes packed an extra apple for the pony. One day Harry was slow offering Blackie his treat, so the little animal stuck his fuzzy nose right into Harry's lunch pail and helped himself.

Many of the ponies, including Blackie, seemed to have a sixth sense about danger in the mines. Once, Blackie refused to go along a passage—and suddenly the roof collapsed right in front of him. Harry came to trust and depend on Blackie's intuition to keep them both safe in the tunnels.

When Harry and the other miners had their two-week holiday every summer, the mines closed down and the ponies had a vacation, too. Blackie and all the ponies were brought up out of the mine. For the first time in almost a year they felt the sun on their backs and smelled the sweet grass. They ran and bucked around the pasture.

This vacation was also a chance for Harry's twin daughters to meet the little animal who kept their dad company all day in the dark tunnels. They brought Blackie carrots, apples, and sometimes even lumps of sugar, and they giggled when his velvety muzzle nuzzled their hands.

END OF AN ERA

Technology continued to change, around the world and in the mines. In the late 1800s, not long after the steam engine that brought the Industrial Revolution, gas and diesel engines were invented. There was less demand for coal and fewer ponies were needed belowground.

Then, in the early 1900s, machines to haul coal out of the mines began to replace ponies. What a change—the pit pony population in Britain was at its peak in 1913, when there were about 70,000 of the little horses underground in mines. But by 1978 there were only 200 pit ponies working in English coal pits.

Blackie worked until he was well into his 20s, although by that point, he was only working four hours a day. He retired to a farm along with Bumble and Pip, but Harry never forgot him. He and his daughters often visited the pony who had once worked so hard—and of course they brought him treats.

There were just 43 pit ponies left in England by 1988. All the little animals were retired shortly after that and most lived out the rest of their lives in animal sanctuaries or on farms where they were well taken care of.

WORKHORSES

Although machinery has replaced horses in many parts of the world, about 100 million horses, donkeys, and mules are still used for farming and transportation in less developed areas—around 27 million work in Africa alone. Horses are

Heavy Horses

The biggest members of the horse family are the *draft,* or *heavy,* horses, and not surprisingly, they can haul the heaviest loads. Breeds such as Belgians, Clydesdales, Friesians, Percherons, and Shires are tall and muscular, with broad, short backs and powerful hind legs.

A draft horse's face often has a straighter nose, or profile, than other breeds of horses. These gentle giants tend to be calm and patient, and make great farm horses, helping with heavy plowing, pulling large wagons, and hauling logs.

Many heavy horses have long, silky hair that grows just above their hooves. This "feather" helps direct rain off the horses' hooves.

Horses and horse mills were used to move heavy mine shaft lifts in the mid-1800s.

Teeny Tiny Horses

Smaller than ponies, but with a horse's slimmer build, miniature horses are friendly and long-lived. They stand only slightly taller than an adult's waist and look quite delicate, but these little creatures—once pampered royal pets in France and other European countries—are very hardy.

Miniature horses used to pull carts in coal mines but now some work as therapy horses. They visit hospitals, providing comfort and giving patients a chance to interact with a gentle animal. Other miniature horses are trained to assist people with disabilities, the same way service dogs do.

The Fallabella miniature horse is one of the smallest horse breeds in the world.

THE LAST MINE IN THE UNITED STATES THAT USED PIT PONIES CLOSED IN 1971.

one of only about 14 large animals that people have domesticated—the others include camels, reindeer, and pigs. Horses make good work animals because they're not too aggressive or flighty, and they're large enough to pull heavy loads, but not too large to control. As well, horses aren't meat eaters, so they don't try to turn their owners into lunch.

Some horses provide the power for grinding grain or pumping water. In a machine known as a horse mill, the horse walks in a circle, turning a mill that crushes ore from a mine or compresses fruit to extract its juice. Other horses are out on woodland trails, clearing them, finding lost hikers, or providing disaster-relief assistance.

Some horses work with people who have special needs. Riding horses can help them develop better balance and physical coordination. Being on horseback gives people who have physical disabilities a chance to be more mobile and to combine being active with bonding with an animal. Riders gain a real sense of achievement when they learn to make a large animal like a horse follow their directions.

Although horses and ponies no long work in coal mines, for many decades ponies like Blackie made a dirty, difficult, dangerous job not only more efficient but also more tolerable, with a nudge of a fuzzy head or a nuzzle from a velvety nose. Now they work at different jobs, less dangerous in many cases, but still essential.

Seabiscuit

A Winner Against All Odds

A cheer went up as the two horses were led onto the racetrack. War Admiral was headstrong and majestic, pulling against the bridle, fighting his groom. Seabiscuit plodded along with his head hanging down. There didn't seem to be much doubt about which one would win this race.

Huge crowds pushed against the rail by the track's grandstand. The race had been billed as the Match of the Century and the air was filled with excitement. Forty million people across the United States—including the president—were glued to their radios, waiting to hear the play-by-play description of the race.

As the horses strode up the track, a hush fell over the crowd. War Admiral and Seabiscuit took their places at the starting line. The two horses were full of nervous energy and had a hard time settling into place.

Then the starting bell rang!

"And they're off," called the racetrack announcer . . .

Seabiscuit and jockey George Woolf made a good team. Woolf's nickname was "The Iceman" because he kept his cool no matter how exciting a race became.

THOROUGHBRED IS A BREED KNOWN FOR SPEED AND SPIRIT. THEY ARE OFTEN RACEHORSES.

THE BISCUIT

Seabiscuit came from champion stock, but you wouldn't have known it to look at him. This runty little bay Thoroughbred had short, stocky legs. His left front leg jabbed out wildly as he ran, and people said he had an odd "egg-beater gait."

How did Seabiscuit get such a strange name? His father's name was Hard Tack, which is also the name for a cracker (or biscuit) that stays edible for a long time, so it was often brought along on lengthy sea voyages. You might say hard tack is a kind of sea biscuit. As well, Seabiscuit's grandmother was named Tea Biscuit, so the name fit.

Many racehorses seem to love running, but not Seabiscuit. No wonder: he lost his first 17 races. As a matter of fact, he raced 35 times as a two-year-old horse—that's more than three times the number of matches most horses that age race—and lost almost every time.

Eccentric but successful trainer Tom Smith first saw Seabiscuit in June 1936 and was convinced the little horse had potential. When Seabiscuit's owner was selling him at a bargain price, Smith convinced his boss, Charles Howard, to buy the Biscuit. "Get me that horse," Smith said to Howard. "He has real stuff in him. I can improve him. I'm positive."

Smith felt that Seabiscuit needed to be treated well before he could develop a love for racing. On Howard's ranch in California, Smith let Seabiscuit eat as much as he wanted, and quieted the horse by introducing into his stall a dog, a spider monkey, and a peaceful old pony. Many race-horses are more comfortable when they have other animals

Galloping Through History

around as companions. Seabiscuit quickly responded to the treatment and seemed to love the racecourse and outrunning other horses.

The horse was allowed to sleep as much as he liked and he would doze for hours. Unlike most horses, Seabiscuit also slept lying down for long stretches.

Seabiscuit was matched with jockey Johnny "Red" Pollard. He was known as Red because of his flaming ginger hair. Like Seabiscuit, Red had had his share of losses and tough breaks, so he felt a special bond with the horse. That bond paid off on the racetrack: with Red in the saddle, Seabiscuit began to win race after race.

"The Biscuit," as he was also called, was soon known as the fastest horse in the western United States. But owner Charles Howard, trainer Tom Smith, and jockey Red were sure he was the fastest horse in America!

THE ADMIRAL

In the eastern United States, the horse that won the most races was War Admiral. Small but high-spirited, this dark-brown horse looked like a champion. No wonder—he was related to Man o' War, one of the greatest Thoroughbred racehorses ever. But then, so was Seabiscuit.

War Admiral and Seabiscuit both set records for speed and won race after race—but they'd never competed against each other. By 1938, horseracing fans were clamoring for the two champions to meet. A race like that would distract everyone from their day-to-day lives. And in the 1930s, most Americans badly needed that.

Zzzzzz!

Seabiscuit was unusual for a horse because he would lie down to sleep for long stretches of time—most horses can only lie down for a few minutes. That's because of their large size and body structure.

A horse can sleep on its feet thanks to "hooks," called stay apparatus, in the kneecaps of its hind legs. These lock the horse's knees and keep it upright, even when asleep. Sleeping on its feet lets a horse make a quick getaway if it feels threatened.

HARD TIMES

In the 1920s, or the Roaring Twenties, there had been wealth, fun, and optimism in the United States and much of the world. People bought and sold investments and believed prices could only go up, and that their stocks and bonds would keep increasing in value.

But on Tuesday, October 29, 1929, the stock market crashed and the American economy began to fail. Millions of people suddenly lost their jobs and their homes. Before long, one out of every four people was unemployed. It was the beginning of the Great Depression, the longest and most devastating economic downturn in modern-day history.

During those dark days, people desperately looked for something to give them hope. North Americans listened to Seabiscuit's races on the radio (there were no televisions in homes then) and avidly read newspaper and magazine stories about him. As they heard more and more about Seabiscuit, the funny-looking little horse who despite so many losses still managed to be a winner, they were inspired. People wanted

To save money during the Depression, drivers hitched up horses to pull their cars. In Canada, vehicles like this one were known as Bennett buggies, after Canada's prime minister, R.B. Bennett. In the United States, people called them Hoover wagons, after American president Herbert Hoover.

a second chance in life, just like Seabiscuit. They felt that if a quirky horse could come from behind to be a champion, then perhaps they could, too.

Horseracing was popular during the Depression because gambling on races had been legalized just shortly before the economic crash. People couldn't find jobs so they had lots of time to attend the races. Some hoped to gamble their way to riches. Perhaps they believed Seabiscuit's luck would rub off on them. By 1938, after suffering through the Depression for nine years, they sure could have used some good luck.

THE MATCH OF THE CENTURY

November 1, 1938, dawned crisp and cool at Pimlico Race Course in Baltimore, Maryland. After days of rain, the sun was shining at last. Still, everyone worried whether the track would be dry enough for the incredible race they'd all been anticipating. At 8:30 that morning, people held their breath as a track expert examined the field. Finally, he made his announcement: the track was fine, and the race would go ahead.

Already the crowds were arriving at the track. By 10:00 a.m.—still more than six hours before race time— thousands of people were banging against the surrounding fences. When the gates opened, they poured in.

At noon the grandstand was full—and the crowds kept coming. From people in thin, threadbare coats to elegantly dressed celebrities and noblemen from foreign countries, more than 40,000 spectators crammed into Pimlico. Thousands even stood in the infield, the oval-shaped area Seabiscuit and War Admiral would be racing around. When the two horses at last made their way onto the track, the crowd was in a frenzy.

RED POLLARD'S NICKNAME FOR SEABISCUIT WAS POP.

Shoes for Horses

Horses originally lived on dry plains and their hooves evolved for life there. But now horses walk on hard race-courses, rough roads, and other challenging surfaces. Many owners feel their horses need to wear metal horseshoes to keep their hooves from wearing unevenly or tearing.

A horse's hooves are made of the same material as your fingernails, so it doesn't hurt to have the shoes nailed onto them. But some people feel that if a horse is fed and cared for correctly, it doesn't need shoes.

Built to Run

Horses don't have sharp claws or teeth, so when danger threatens, their best defense is to run. And they're good at it. Horses walk and run on their tiptoes, not their whole foot as humans do, which makes their long strides even longer.

The bones and muscles of a horse's legs are built for forward and backward strides. Horses also have muscles that help them store up energy between strides. As well, running pumps a horse's lungs to make breathing easier.

Red had been injured so his friend George Woolf was riding Seabiscuit. Woolf had met with Red for hours before the race, finding out how to motivate Seabiscuit, and coming up with a strategy for winning, based on Red's experience with the little horse.

Seabiscuit and War Admiral, who had his regular jockey, Charley Kurtsinger, on board, headed toward their starting positions. Woolf turned Seabiscuit's head so he could take a good look at War Admiral. One of the things Red had told Woolf was that the Biscuit seemed to run faster when he knew who his opponent was.

And then the starting flag flashed down, the bell rang, and the race began. War Admiral was famous for being quick off the mark but Seabiscuit surprised the crowd by springing forward at the same instant. Woolf and Tom Smith, Seabiscuit's trainer, had secretly prepared their horse to burst from the starting line as soon as he heard the bell. The two horses tore down the track, side by side. Each ran faster and faster, but neither could get in front of the other.

Then a gasp went up from the crowd. They watched in amazement as Seabiscuit pulled ahead of War Admiral. They saw Seabiscuit's nose inch past his opponent, then his head and neck. Soon Seabiscuit was completely in front of War Admiral, with no sign of slowing down.

"Seabiscuit is outrunning him!" cried the shocked track announcer. It was clear that War Admiral was having trouble keeping up.

Galloping Through History

FROM THE CALVERT·LITHO·CO., DETROIT, MICH.

The huge crowd was so frantic that it broke down a long stretch of the infield fencing. Within seconds, the mob surged toward the railing alongside the track. They yelled and waved at the horses but Seabiscuit didn't seem to notice. Woolf let Seabiscuit get even farther ahead of War Admiral—5 meters (16 feet), or about the length of two horses.

Although War Admiral had lost his quick-start advantage, he was running well and his jockey still felt he could win. The Admiral had great staying power and Kurtsinger assessed that Seabiscuit was running much too fast too early on for so tough a race. So Kurtsinger decided on a new strategy: he'd let Seabiscuit exhaust himself, then War Admiral would roar out in front at the last minute.

The Forgotten Jockeys

In the late 1800s, there were many African-American jockeys. Back in 1875, at the first Kentucky Derby, one of American horse racing's biggest events, almost all of the riders were African-Americans. They were good, too—black jockeys won 15 of the first 28 runnings of the Kentucky Derby.

But because of racism and resentful white jockeys, black jockeys were blocked from riding. Between 1921 and 2000, none took part in the Kentucky Derby. Attitudes have changed, and slowly black jockeys are returning to horse racing.

Record Setters

The fastest a horse has ever run in a race on a racetrack was 70.76 kilometers (43.97 miles) per hour . The horse was named Winning Brew and he set the record in 2008. Don't forget he was also carrying a jockey on his back at the time!

However, most experts would say Secretariat, shown above, was the best overall racehorse ever. In the early 1970s he won many races and usually set records doing it.

NECK AND NECK AGAIN

Kurtsinger let Seabiscuit keep the lead. He moved War Admiral right in behind the other horse, to maintain the pressure, and bided his time.

The two horses chased each other down the track. Woolf taunted Kurtsinger by yelling back to him, "Hey, get on up here with me! We're supposed to have a horse race here! What are you doing lagging back there?"

Going into the straightaway, Kurtsinger began to make his move. War Admiral bounded forward, cutting into Seabiscuit's lead. Stride by stride, the Admiral crept up until the two horses were again neck and neck.

Kurtsinger was positive it would be another win for his horse.

The tension in the crowd was incredible and the grandstand was shaking. People screamed with excitement as the horses pounded down the track. Some fans jumped up and down, others fainted.

But Seabiscuit still hadn't reached his top speed. He refused to let War Admiral pass him so the two horses dashed along beside each other as they came into the final turn.

Kurtsinger was pushing War Admiral with all his strength. The two horses seemed to glare at each other and Seabiscuit's ears flattened. He was desperate to win this race but now War Admiral was inching ahead.

THE HOME STRETCH

Woolf urged Seabiscuit onward one last time. Somehow, the horse found the strength to surge ahead. War Admiral kept up with Seabiscuit for a few strides but just couldn't sustain the pace. He began to fall back as Seabiscuit continued to tear down the track.

"So long, Charley," said Woolf as his horse pulled away. Soon Seabiscuit was ahead by the length of his whole body, then two lengths. And he just kept going.

"Seabiscuit by three," screamed the announcer. "Seabiscuit by three!"

War Admiral struggled to catch up but it was too late. Seabiscuit won the race by an astounding four lengths. The Match of the Century had been won in record time by the little horse that almost no one thought could be a winner. The crowd went wild.

YOU CAN WATCH SEABISCUIT'S EXCITING RACE AGAINST WAR ADMIRAL ONLINE.

RACING THROUGH HISTORY

No one remembers when the first horse race took place or why, but it was at least 3,700 years ago and people loved the sport from the beginning. Chariot races were first included in the Olympics back in 684 BCE. About 40 years later, horseback riders began to compete in the games.

Two thousand years ago in Rome, almost everyone went to the chariot races, and Roman charioteers were heroes. Then horse racing dropped from popularity for almost 1,000 years. It didn't come back into fashion until 1660, when King Charles II of England encouraged the people in his court to ride and compete against each other. Horse racing quickly spread to other nations and today horse races are held in more than 50 countries.

There are many different types of races. There is flat racing, on a track, like what Seabiscuit did, and racing with jumps included, which is called jump racing or steeplechasing.

The crowd went wild when, near the end of the race, War Admiral was less than a length behind Seabiscuit.

In harness racing, horses pull a light, two-wheeled vehicle called a sulky.

People compete on horseback in many other ways. Dressage is the art of training a horse to perform precise maneuvers. In show jumping, horses and riders have to ride over jumps of different types and heights. Endurance riding involves a course as long as 160 kilometers (100 miles). In the game of polo, players on horseback use mallets to drive a ball into the opposing team's goal.

SEABISCUIT'S LEGACY

The Great Depression ended in 1939 with the beginning of World War II. Even though the U.S. had not yet entered the war, suddenly there were lots of jobs: soldier, plane builder, ammunition-factory worker, and more. Laws were set up to prevent such a crash from ever happening again and governments established programs to help people who were still struggling with poverty.

Seabiscuit and War Admiral's Match of the Century is still considered the best horse race ever. People will never forget the little horse that inspired the world and helped people cope with the tragedy of the Great Depression. Seabiscuit's career had a bad start, but what a turnaround he had! When he finally retired he was racing's all-time top money winner.

One More Time

Racing is one way riders interact with their horses. Another is by reenacting famous events, such as American Revolution battles, medieval knights' clashes, or pioneer conflicts. Reenactment horses have to be calm and good-natured because they'll have to cope with flags flapping, "soldiers" yelling, music blaring, and drums banging.

Depending on the era being reenacted, horses may also have to cope with musket fire, the smell of gunpowder, cannons booming, or armor clanking. Horses have to wear the correct saddle and bridle for the period and the rider's rank.

TIME LINE

BCE

50 million years ago	*Eohippus*, the earliest ancestor of the horse family, evolves in North America
5 million years ago	*Equus*, the modern horse, appears
3500	People begin riding horses
3000	The first wheeled vehicles pulled by horses
2500	Soldiers in southern Russia and west-central Asia ride into battle in two-wheeled chariots
900	Soldiers learn to fight on horseback
750	Saddles invented in Assyria
600	Cyrus the Great of Persia sets up a postal system using horses to deliver messages
500	Stirrups invented
344	Alexander the Great meets Bucephalus
323	Alexander the Great dies
100	Horse collar invented; allows horses to pull heavy vehicles
10	Romans develop mail system using light carriages pulled by fast horses

CE

1200s	
early 1200s	Genghis Khan leads Mongol soldiers on horseback to create huge empire
late 1200s	Knights begin wearing armor for battle
1300s	
1300s	Invention of gunpowder changes the role of the warhorse
1400s	
1493	Christopher Columbus brings horses to the New World

1500s	
early 1500s	**Spanish exploration of North America**
1600s	
late 1600s	**Horses pull the first taxis in Paris**
1700s	
1700s	**People travel between European towns in regularly scheduled horse-drawn coaches**
1775	**American Revolution begins**
1777 Star	**Sybil Ludington makes her famous ride on her horse,**
1783	**America wins the revolution; becomes independent from Britain**
late 1700s	**Industrial Revolution in Europe**
1800s	
1819	**Horses pull the first buses in Paris**
1842	**Pit ponies begin hauling coal out of mines**
early 1860s	**Expansion of American West**
1860	**Pony Express begins**
1861	**American Civil War begins**
1861	**Pony Express's last official delivery**
late 1800s	**Horses begin to be replaced by the car**
1900s	
1913	**About 70,000 pit ponies work in Britain's coal mines**
early 1900s	**Machines begin to replace pit ponies in mines**
1914	**World War I breaks out, the last major battle conflict in which warhorses are used**
1929	**U.S. stock market crash begins the Great Depression**
1938	**Seabiscuit races War Admiral in the Match of the Century**
1971	**Last mine in the United States using pit ponies closes**
1979	**Mustangs are designated as an endangered species**

TIME LINE

HORSING AROUND: HORSEY PLACES TO VISIT

Bucephalus

British Museum, London, England
Naples National Archaeological Museum, Naples, Italy

Mustangs

International Museum of the Horse, Lexington, Kentucky
Maritime Museum of the Atlantic, Halifax, Nova Scotia
Museum of Natural History, Halifax, Nova Scotia

Sybil Ludington

American Independence Museum, Exeter, New Hampshire
Monument, Carmel, New York (smaller versions of the statue are at the Daughters of the
        American Revolution Headquarters in Washington, DC; at the public library in
        Danbury, Connecticut; and at the Elliot and Rosemary Offner Sculpture Learning
        and Research Center at Brookgreen Gardens, Murrells Inlet, South Carolina)
Roadside markers along the route of Sybil Ludington's historic ride, Putnam County,
        New York

Pony Express

Fort Laramie National Historic Site, Fort Laramie, Wyoming
Hollenberg Pony Express Station State Historic Site, Hanover, Kansas
Pony Express National Museum, St. Joseph, Missouri
Rock Creek Station State Historical Park, Fairbury, Nebraska
Wells Fargo History Museum, Old Sacramento State Historic Park, Sacramento, California

Pit Ponies

Beamish Museum, Beamish, County Durham, England
Cape Breton Miners' Museum, Glace Bay, Nova Scotia
National Coal Mining Museum, Caphouse Colliery, Overton, England

Seabiscuit

The National Museum of Racing and Hall of Fame, Saratoga Springs, New York
Remington Carriage Museum, Cardston, Alberta
Seabiscuit Statue, Santa Anita Park, Arcadia, California

MAIN SOURCES

Bucephalus

Ann Hyland. *The Horse in the Ancient World*. Westport, CT: Praeger, 2003.

Plutarch. *The Age of Alexander*. London: Penguin Books, 1973.

Monty Roberts. *The Man Who Listens to Horses*. Toronto: Vintage Canada, 1998.

Mustangs

Johanna Bertin. *Sable Island*. Canmore, AB: Altitude Publishing Canada, 2006.

Lyall Campbell. *Sable Island, Fatal and Fertile Crescent*. Windsor, NS: Lancelot Press Ltd., 1974.

Caroline Davis. *The Kingdom of the Horse*. Willowdale, ON: Firefly Books Ltd., 1998.

Hope Ryden. *America's Last Wild Horses*. Guilford, CT: Lyons Press, 2005.

J. Edward de Steiguer. *Wild Horses of the West*. Tucson, AZ: University of Arizona Press, 2011.

Deanne Stillman. *Mustang*. New York: Houghton Mifflin Co., 2008.

Sybil Ludington

Alan Axelrod. *The Real History of the American Revolution: A New Look at the Past*. New York: Sterling, 2007.

Carol Berkin. *Revolutionary Mothers*. New York: Alfred A. Knopf, 2005.

V.T. Dacquino. *Sybil Ludington: The Call to Arms*. Fleischmanns, NY: Purple Mountain Press, Ltd., 2000.

Esther Forbes. *Paul Revere and the World He Lived In*. Boston: Houghton Mifflin, 1999.

Melissa Lukeman Bohrer. *Glory, Passion, and Principle*. New York: Atria Books, 2003.

Pony Express

Glenn Danford Bradley. *The Story of the Pony Express*. San Francisco: Hesperian House, 1960.

Christopher Corbett. *Orphans Preferred: The Twisted Truth And Lasting Legend of the Pony Express*. New York: Broadway Books, 2003.

C.W. Guthrie. *The Pony Express: An Illustrated History*. Guilford, CT: TwoDot Books, 2010.

Fred Reinfeld. *Pony Express*. Lincoln, NB: University of Nebraska Press, 1973.

Pit Ponies

Stephen Budiansky. *The Nature of Horses*. New York: The Free Press, 1997.

J. Edward Chamberlin. *Horse: How the Horse Has Shaped Civilizations*. Toronto: Alfred A. Knopf, 2006.

Ann Norton Greene. *Horses at Work*. Cambridge, MA: Harvard University Press, 2008.

Seabiscuit

Nicholas Clee. *Eclipse*. London: Transworld Publishers, 2011.

Laura Hillenbrand. *Seabiscuit: An American Legend*. New York: Random House, 2001.

H. Paul Jeffers. *The Great Depression*. Indianapolis, IN: Alpha Books, 2002.

Lionel Robbins. *The Great Depression*. New Brunswick, NJ: Transaction Publishers, 2009.

Steve Wiegand. *Lessons for the Great Depression*. Hoboken, NJ: Wiley Publishing, Inc., 2009.

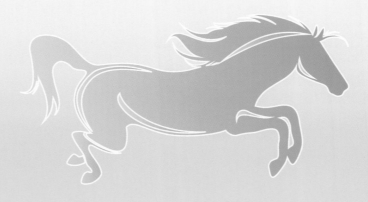

FURTHER READING

Bucephalus

Juliet Clutton-Brock. *Horse*. New York: DK Publishing, Inc., 2008.

Suzanne Jurmain. *Once Upon a Horse*. New York: Lothrop, Lee & Shepard Books, 1989.

Katherine Roberts. *I Am the Great Horse*. New York: The Chicken House, 2006.

Mustangs

Elwyn Hartley Edwards. *The Ultimate Horse Book*. Scarborough, ON: Prentice-Hall Canada, 1991.

Wendy Kitts. *Sable Island: The Wandering Sandbar*. Halifax, NS: Nimbus Publishing, 2011.

David Murdoch. *Cowboy*. New York: DK Publishing, Inc., 2000.

———. *North American Indian*. New York: DK Publishing, Inc., 2005.

Gail B. Stewart. *Mustangs and Wild Horses*. Minneapolis, MN: Capstone Press, 1996.

Sybil Ludington

Cheryl Harness. *Remember the Ladies: 100 Great American Women*. New York: HarperCollins, 2001.

Phillip Hoose. *We Were There, Too! Young People in U.S. History*. New York: Melanie Kroupa Books, Farrar, Straus and Giroux, 2001.

Connie Solano. *Courageous Women: Thirty-Two Short Stories*. Tucson, AZ: Wheatmark, Inc., 2010.

Marlene Targ Brill. *Extraordinary Young People*. New York: Children's Press, 1996.

Pony Express

Cheryl Harness. *They're Off!: The Story of the Pony Express*. New York: Simon & Schuster Books for Young Readers, 1996.

Steven Kroll. *Pony Express!* New York: Scholastic, 1996.

John Woodward. *Horses: The Ultimate Treasury*. New York: DK Publishing, Inc., 2012.

Pit Ponies

Joyce Barkhouse. *Pit Pony*. Halifax, NS: Formac Publishing Company, 2010.

Kathy Elgin. *The Great Depression*. Chicago: World Book, Inc., 2011.

Monica Halpern. *Moving North*. Washington, DC: National Geographic Society, 2006.

Seabiscuit

Kathy Elgin. *The Great Depression*. Chicago: World Book, Inc., 2011.

Mona Gedney. *The Story of the Great Depression*. Hockessin, DE: Mitchell Lane Publishers, 2005.

Ralph Moody. *Come On Seabiscuit!* Greenwich, CT: Bison Books Corp., 2003.

Sheila Nelson. *Crisis at Home and Abroad: The Great Depression, World War II and Beyond*. Philadelphia: Mason Crest Publishers, Inc., 2006.

Peggy J. Parks. *The Great Depression*. Farmington Hills, MI: KidHaven Press, 2004.

Peter Roop. *Tales of Famous Animals*. New York: Scholastic Reference, 2012.

PHOTO CREDITS

INDEX

Afghanistan, 12, 38
Alexander the Great, 1–12, 72
American Civil War, 11, 48, 50, 73
American Revolutionary War, 26, 27, 28, 36, 71, 73
armies, 1, 5, 7, 9, 10, 11, 32
armor, 9, 11, 71, 72
arrows, 4, 18, 19, 20, 21
Asia, 8, 10, 11, 21, 37, 49, 72
Assateague horses, 24
Assyria, 6, 72
Australia, 20, 32, 53

barges, 33
battle, 1, 6, 7, 8, 9, 11, 12, 28, 29, 30, 34, 35, 36, 71, 72
Battle of Ridgefield, 35, 36
Battle of the River Hydaspes, 8
bay, 5, 35, 44, 47, 62
Belgians, 53, 59
Belgium, 53
Blackfoot, 13–25
bridles, 4, 7, 17, 23, 55, 61, 71
Britain, 36, 58, 73
Bucephalus, 1–12, 72
buffalo, 10, 13–24, 44, 49
"Buffalo Bill," 46, 47
buses, 33, 73
bushrangers, 32

Canada, 24, 53, 64
cantinas, 41
carriages, 36, 49, 72
cars, 12, 36, 37, 38, 56, 64, 73
carts, 12, 30, 37, 51, 52, 55, 57, 60
cavalry, 2, 7, 8, 11, 12
centaurs, 5
chariots, 10, 11, 70, 72
chestnut, 25
Cheyenne people, 25
China, 8, 30
Chincoteague Ponies, 24, 25
Clydesdales, 59
coaches, 33, 38, 49, 73. *See also* stagecoaches
coal, 51–60, 73
Columbus, Christopher, 18, 72
Comanche people, 25
Connecticut, 27, 28, 36
Cortés, Hernán, 18
Crow people, 25
Cyrus the Great, 49, 72

Danbury, 28, 31, 35, 36
de Soto, Hernando, 18
Dominican Republic, 18
donkeys, 38, 53, 55, 59
draft horses, 53, 59
dressage, 71

Egypt, 12, 55
endangered species, 21, 25, 73
endurance riding, 71
England, 11, 32, 49, 52, 53, 59, 70
Eohippus, 15, 72
Equus, 72, 72

farmers, 22, 31, 37
farriers, 55
feathers, 59
forelocks, 31
France, 11, 53, 60
Fredericksburg, 36
Friesians, 53, 59
Frontier Nursing Service, 58
Fry, Johnny, 44–45, 47

game wardens, 38
Germany, 8, 53
Great Depression, 64, 71, 73
Great Plain, 24
Great Wall of China, 8
Greece, 12
grooms, 1, 53, 54, 61, 64
gunpowder, 11, 71, 72

Hamilton, Billy, 41, 47
hands, 47, 48
harnesses, 30
hauling, 10, 12, 23, 52, 57, 58, 59, 73
heavy horses, 59
highwaymen, 32
Holy Dogs, 25
home stations, 44
horse collars, 30, 72
horse mills, 59, 60
horsepower, 56
horseshoes, 53, 55, 56, 65
horse whispering, 4
horses,
        breeds, 45, 59, 60, 62
        buffalo, 13, 14, 17, 18, 20, 22

eyes, 19, 54, 56
feet, 55, 63, 66
feral, 20, 21
hearing, 25
hooves, 6, 14, 21, 59, 65
legs, 14, 16, 48, 54, 59, 66
noses, 23, 59
pack, 20
sense of smell, 25
sleep, 63
vision, 19, 25, 54, 56
wild, 21, 22, 24, 25. *See also* mustangs
Howard, Charles, 62, 63, 64
Huns, 8, 11

Industrial Revolution, 52, 58, 73

jockeys, 62, 63, 64, 66, 67, 68
        African-American, 67

Kentucky Derby, 67
Khan, Genghis, 8, 9, 72
knights, 9, 11, 71, 72
Kurtsinger, Charley, 66, 67, 68, 69

Lakota people, 25
Lincoln, Abraham, 47, 48
Ludington, Sybil, 26, 27, 28, 30–38
Ludingtonville, 36

Macedonia, 2, 4, 12
mail, 39–45, 47, 49, 50, 72
Man o' War, 63
manes, 5, 17, 21, 25, 31, 35, 48
mares, 13, 14, 25, 44
Match of the Century, the, 61, 65, 69, 71, 73
Mesohippus, 15
Mexico, 18
militia, 28, 29, 30, 32, 34, 35
mines, 51–60, 73
miniature horses, 60
mochila, 41, 42, 44, 45, 50
Mongols, 8, 9, 11, 72
morgans, 45
mules, 10, 38, 50, 55, 57, 59
mustangs, 13–25, 45, 73

National Pony Express Association (NPEA), 50
Native people, 16, 19, 22, 23, 24, 25, 49

INDEX

natural horsemanship, 4
North America, 13, 15, 18, 22, 23, 24, 25, 32, 46, 64, 72
Nova Scotia, 24, 53
nurses, 58

Paiute people, 49
Pakistan, 8, 11
Paris, 33, 73
park rangers, 38
Patriots, 26, 28, 33, 34, 35, 38
Pegasus, 5
Percherons, 53, 59
Persia, 10, 49, 72
Philip of Macedonia, King, 1–6
pintos, 25, 45
pit ponies, 51–60, 73
plowing, 10, 59
police, 32
Pollard, Johnny "Red," 63, 64, 65, 66
polo, 7, 71
ponies, 24, 25, 30, 48, 51–60, 73. *See also* Pony Express
Pony Express, 39–50, 73
Przewalski's horses, 21

racehorses, 9, 61–71
racing, 9, 61–71, 73
racism, 67
ranches, 25, 62
Randall, James, 40, 41, 44
reenactments, 46, 50, 71
relay stations, 40, 44, 49
Revere, Paul, 28
riding, 2, 30, 36, 37, 60, 72
Rising, Don, 45
running, 62, 63, 67
Russia, 7, 8, 10, 21, 37, 72

Sable Island Ponies, 24
Sacramento, 41, 47
saddles, 2, 6, 7, 17, 23, 35, 41, 45, 71, 72
San Francisco, 40, 44, 47
Seabiscuit, 61–71, 73
Secretariat, 68
Shetland ponies, 51, 52
Shires, 59
show jumping, 71
sidesaddle, 35–36
Sioux people, 25
Sky Dogs, 17
Smith, Tom, 62, 63, 64, 66

soldiers, 2, 6, 8, 10, 11, 12, 26, 28, 29, 31, 32, 33, 34, 35, 71, 72
Spain, 18, 22
St. Joseph, 44, 47
stables, 7, 53, 55, 56, 57, 64
stagecoaches, 38, 40, 44, 46, 47
Star, 26, 27, 30–37, 73
stations. *See* home stations, relay stations
stay apparatus, 63
steeplechasing, 70
stirrups, 2, 10, 72
sulkies, 71
Sybil, Daughter of the American Revolution, 36

taxis, 33, 73
telegraph, 40, 45, 48, 49, 50
tepees, 20, 23, 24
therapy horses, 60
thieves, 7, 26, 32, 35
Thoroughbreds, 45, 62, 63
trainers, 62, 63, 64, 66
trains, 32, 37, 44, 45, 49
travois, 17, 23, 24
tribes, 11, 13, 14, 18, 20, 22, 23, 24, 25
Trojan Horse, 5

United States of America, 27, 28, 35, 40, 45, 53, 60, 61, 63, 64, 73
Upson, Warren, 42–44

wagons, 30, 52, 59, 64
War Admiral, 61, 63, 65, 66, 67, 68, 69, 70, 71, 73
warfare, 1, 6, 10, 11, 12, 23, 26, 27, 28, 34, 36, 48, 49, 50, 71, 72, 73
warhorses, 1–12
Washington, George, 35
weapons, 2, 4, 6, 8, 11, 12, 18, 23, 29, 33, 34, 35, 71
Winning Brew, 68
withers, 47
women, 6, 17, 23, 34, 35, 36, 52
Woolf, George, 62, 66, 67, 68, 69
work horses, 51–60, 73
world wars, 11, 12, 34, 71, 73

ACKNOWLEDGMENTS

Many thanks to the Beach/Schriver family for your interest in this book. I truly appreciate your support and generosity.

It was wonderful to work again with editor Chandra Wohleber, who made sure I never put the cart before the horse in my manuscript. As ever, I also loved horsing around with designer Sheryl Shapiro and photo researcher Sandra Booth—thank you for the many ways you improved this book.

Keeping the process of this book's creation going at a good, steady trot was managing editor Katie Hearn—thank you! I'm also very grateful to proofreader Eleanor Gasparik and copyeditor Linda Pruessen. Thanks as well to Brigitte Waisberg, marketing manager, and the entire Annick team.

I also appreciated the help of the librarians of the Toronto Public Library system, especially those at the Leaside Library and the Toronto Reference Library.

Thanks always to Dad, John, and Douglas, definitely horses of a different color! Special thanks and love to Paul—and that's straight from the horse's mouth!